Good Grief,
Pass the Bread,
Mom Is Dead

Good Grief, Pass the Bread, Mom Is Dead

A Memoir

Angela Nissel

AMISTAD

An Imprint of HarperCollins*Publishers*

The names and identifying characteristics of some of the individuals featured throughout this book have been changed to protect their privacy.

HarperCollins books may be purchased for educational, business, or sales promotional use. For information, please email the Special Markets Department at SPsales@harpercollins.com.

hc.com

FIRST EDITION

Designed by Jason Kayser

Library of Congress Cataloging-in-Publication Data
Names: Nissel, Angela, 1974- author
Title: Good grief, pass the bread, Mom is dead / Angela Nissel.
Description: New York, NY : Amistad, 2026.
Identifiers: LCCN 2025009726 (print) | LCCN 2025009727 (ebook) | ISBN 9780063345119 trade paperback | ISBN 9780063345133 ebook
Subjects: LCSH: Nissel, Angela, 1974—Family | Breast—Cancer—Patients—Family relationships | Women caregivers—United States—Biography | Women authors—United States—Biography | Terminally ill parents—United States | Mothers and daughters—United States | Grief | LCGFT: Autobiographies
Classification: LCC RC280.B8 N55 2026 (print) | LCC RC280.B8 (ebook)
LC record available at https://lccn.loc.gov/2025009726
LC ebook record available at https://lccn.loc.gov/2025009727

Printed in the United States of America

26 27 28 29 30 LBC 5 4 3 2 1

Dedicated to my mother. I love you. This is the last book I embarrass you in. I promise.

All right, we did not die today! I call that an unqualified success!

—*Inside Out*

Contents

Contents

Prologue

At thirty-five, divorced and unemployed, my only full-time job became saving my mother's life. I entered her breast cancer fight armed with little more than the hope promised on her pink ribbon key chain. I was certain we'd soon have a pink "Cancer Survivor" shirt to match.

I knew my mom was just as strong as anyone. Even better, she was that stealth type of strong that could cut someone down to size without cursing, as her disappointed facial expressions were enough to make you feel fully cussed out. I, on the other hand, had no problem with actually cursing people out. Combined, I knew we had the grit to put up a hell of a fight against cancer.

For years, my mom hid how bad her cancer was; she didn't want my help fighting it. She insisted her breast cancer was no big deal, something that would be zapped away through modern medicine as easily as a mole. I believed her, because my mom didn't lie. Turns out, like most good moms, she could tell a whopper of a lie when she felt a lie would protect her children. For my mom, protecting her children from adult problems was as important as keeping Sunday for Jesus. Needing her children's help, to her, was a sin. Whenever I'd ask if there was anything I could do to help her deal with her cancer, she'd always tell me she was fine. She'd remind me that she was tough and had hurdled obstacles my generation only read about in books. That she was only two generations removed from slavery and the daughter of a woman forced to drop out of sixth grade to become a domestic. Despite that, my mom had, in her twenties, earned an Ivy League degree while both marching for civil rights and volunteering for the Black Panthers. Meanwhile, in my twenties, I spent a good deal of time locked in a psych ward volunteering to teach my new fellow patients how to cut hospital steak with a spork.

When I finally beat back the gray clouds of depression, I desperately wanted to make Mom proud. She always told me I could achieve even more than she had, and for a while, I did. For a bit, I was her wildest dream; I moved to California, I had a career, a husband, and a house with a literal picket fence. She would show off about my Los Angeles life in front of her friends, but quietly, I felt I could never measure up to her, to what she expected me to be. Despite my success making her proud, the small rebellious things I did embarrassed her. She seemed to think every choice I made that she didn't agree with was a reflection of how she failed as a mother. One of the rare times she raised her voice was over a tattoo I got when I was thirty. It was a bamboo plant. To me the tattoo had deep meaning, that I could be as tough as she was, yet still bend like bamboo.

"It's like you're trying to embarrass me! Why would you get drugs tattooed on your arm?" she asked.

That's the day I learned I would definitely never measure up to my perfect mom who evidently made it through the sixties without even learning what marijuana looked like. She refused to believe my bamboo tattoo was not the devil's lettuce, so on trips home, no matter the weather, I wore long sleeve shirts so she wouldn't be embarrassed by the weed tattoo that wasn't.

Even before I forced my way into her cancer battle, our relationship was a series of generation-gapped mother-daughter tiffs over everything from tattoos to religion to whether proper women still wore pantyhose. I saw her as overly cautious. My mom saw me as a bit too reckless and overconfident; I was always making life even more complicated by veering off a straight and narrow path, the one she and others had blazed to make life easier for those who came after them.

After I moved away and our talks were mostly over the phone, we often kept them at a surface level, which was easier than spending our precious phone time debating what she once jokingly referred to as my "hippie godless California life." I'd ask her what was new at work. She'd ask me what was new at mine. I'd tell her only the parts of my life I knew would impress her. She'd tell me she was enjoying middle age and all the simple things it taught her to enjoy: a good meal, her new grandson, a random catch-up call from me.

My mom knew she was sharing her cancer battle with a daughter who probably wouldn't handle it as quietly and gracefully as she did. She was absolutely right. When she tossed me that baton, I dropped it often and spectacularly. I moved her to my godless Hollywood life where I learned I knew almost nothing about breast cancer beyond the color pink. Still, despite my many faux pas, the time we spent together fighting cancer was one of the first times she got to see me not as her rebellious tattooed daughter, but as a daughter who had, despite appearances, learned every lesson she'd tried to teach me. We were mismatched buddy cops determined to bring cancer down. We were two adult women, who, for one of the few times in our lives, had a common enemy.

I learned that, despite grit and the best of intentions, everyone can't be a cancer survivor. I also had to learn just as quickly what it meant to give my mom a good death and then, as a bonus prize, learned that despite hard cancer fights and good deaths, grief could still kick my ass. I was as naive about grief as I was about cancer. I knew grief had stages: denial, anger, bargaining, depression, and acceptance but naively thought, *Shit, I got this, I cycle through all those emotions in one hour*. I didn't know grief could be lonely. That it changes your dynamic with the world. I naively thought that people would be as open to talking about death and loss as they were to share the details of their children's births. I knew about substances that came out of my friends' bodies when they brought new life into the world. I knew they went to prenatal classes where other mothers gave them tips and often pitched in to help. Meanwhile, when faced with the opposite end of life, I learned the world doesn't offer classes or community. It just shoves you out the door and wishes you "good luck." If I even hinted at my mother's death in conversations, I felt as if I was wearing a black hooded cloak and carrying a scythe. I learned that birth talk makes for good dinner talk; good deaths, not so much.

I knew that even if my friends didn't understand, my brother and

I would be there for each other after my mom's death. I was wrong. I knew the only way for grief to get better was to give it time. I was wrong. I knew that being the person in charge of her will was an honor. I was very, very wrong. I'd burst into tears dealing with poorly trained chatbots who thought I was threatening them when I used the *d*-word.

> **Chatbot:** How can I help you today?
> **Me:** I want to cancel my mom's credit card. She died.
> **Chatbot:** Don't say that to me.

Around one hundred and twenty people will be gone from the earth in the time it takes to read this page, but I didn't, like most people, think about death until it came for someone I loved. I wish more people felt comfortable with the idea that preparing to have a good death can also be part of a good life. I wish more people knew that in between the periods of grief and desperation are also moments of deep insight and joy. I wish I had been prepared when I was shoved out that door and wished "good luck," but I also believe people learn best when others are brave enough to share their biggest mistakes. Perhaps stories of my unemployed ass believing I was smarter than every oncologist are my contributions to that genre.

Still, as much as I stumbled, with the gift of both time and perspective, I recognize that all I learned from the start of our cancer battle to surviving the years without my mom made me finally understand how my friends could laugh when they shared details of their messy deliveries. Being a human in a meat sack with an expiration date is often overwhelming. The comfort of humor can help get us through the messiness of it all—from the beginning of life to helping someone face the end of it.

So, let's start at the beginning, shall we? Our mother-daughter journey began like so many other stories of women forced to lean on one another: Because one of us realized we'd messed up and married the wrong damn man.

1

Three Christmases and Two Fewer Boobs

Follow the neon signs," my mom instructed me. Those neon arrows pointed the way to a gaudy off-Strip Vegas wedding chapel. The chapel's budget clearly had been spent on their neon billboards as their interior decor consisted solely of plastic floral garlands, each strand strategically placed to hide the chapel's chipped paint. A tall man of about sixty greeted us. He was very shiny. From the sheen of his pomaded hair to his 100 percent rhinestone suit, every part of him sparkled under the fluorescent lights. He was the officiant.

"Did I accidentally book the Elvis package?" my mom whispered after the bedazzled officiant walked off.

The hell if I knew what she booked. The hell if I knew what to make of many of her choices since she'd started dating Bill, the man she was there to marry. My mom liked Elvis about as much as most Black women her age did, which is not at all. Still, if she had booked the Elvis package, I wouldn't have been that shocked. After all, I was in Sin City watching my die-hard Christian mom marry a man she'd met less than a year earlier.

Before meeting Bill, my mom had never been to Vegas. Hell, she'd only been on two other dates that my brother, Jack, and I can remember. That she'd only had two dates was probably partially because my brother and I were so protective. Before one date took her to the movies, we'd grilled him about his life ("So, did you always want to be a security guard?") and wrote down his license plate number before he drove off with our mom.

But her sudden spontaneity was part of what I treasured about her being in love. She was spicing up her life instead of walking that straight-edged line that only went from church to home to work. Before Bill, she was a mom who, on our cross-country catch-up calls, always insisted she was fine. Nope, she wasn't a lonely empty nester; she had my brother, his wife, and her grandson just a few miles away. No need to worry about her, she was blessed and had all she needed. Her happiness was found in simplicity: writing poems about Jesus, buying accessories with Jesus's name on them and then wearing them when she saw Jesus on Sunday. After a few weeks with Bill, she'd morphed from middle-aged into a lovestruck teen. On our weekly phone calls, instead of sharing her poems, she'd started sharing the details of their latest date.

"He took me to Applebee's," she'd said, in a tone that suggested Applebee's was some top-tier dining. I thought that was adorable. Meanwhile, I'd recently eaten at a five-hundred-dollar-a-plate private club in Beverly Hills.

"I like him so much," she'd said. "I gave up an extra shift just to be able to go on a third date with Bill!"

"No, you didn't turn down an extra shift," I'd teased. For my mom, turning down extra work was akin to missing church. I knew a series of penance-based poems would soon be incoming.

"Oh, yes, I did. Turned it right down," Mom replied, once again all gushing and giggly.

Besides her spontaneity, there were other benefits to her being in middle-age love. Shortly before she met Bill on "a Christian chat line, but please tell people we met through friends" my mom had confessed how guilty she felt about not being able to find more time in her sixty-hour workweek to care for her elderly father, my pop-pop. Bill had even fixed that.

"Did I tell you Bill was a reverend?" my mom asked.

She had. She literally reminded me of that every phone call. That was my mom's way of letting me plainly know she didn't plan to do any Bill background checks because God had already done his own. Then she told me Reverend Bill gave Pop-Pop Holy Communion and that Pop-Pop opened his eyes for the first time in weeks and I wanted to say, *I'd open my damn eyes too if a stranger suddenly shoved a cracker in my mouth. Like, wtf?* But I knew Mom wasn't stupid, so I wasn't going to question her ability to pick a boyfriend. Doing that as a daughter felt like teetering over that disrespect line. I simply reasoned that Reverend Bill probably knew more about Communion wafer safety than I did. Plus, I loved hearing my mom sound so carefree, putting herself first for once.

"I've been thinking, if Pop-Pop passes, it's because he knows Bill will take care of me just like he did," my mom had confided.

Pop-Pop did pass and when I flew home for the funeral, Mom assured me she was her favorite word: *fine.* A few weeks later, she definitely seemed to be.

"Bill and I are eloping to Vegas," she'd said. "Don't tell anyone! I wanted to tell you because Las Vegas is pretty close to Los Angeles, right? Maybe you can fly out?" I didn't ask why she didn't want me to tell anyone, I was just proud to be the one chosen to keep her secret. Perhaps the real reason she didn't tell anyone else was that most people her age might know you're not supposed to make any major life decisions like getting freakin' married right after a parent has died.

But I didn't know things like that back then, so I ended up following the neon signs to the gaudy chapel. My then-husband Reggie and I were the sole witnesses to my mom and Reverend Bill's wedding. Soon after the wedding, our mother-daughter calls were all about the fun of her newlywed life. She was a preacher's wife. She had a dedicated parking space at church. She was going to buy a house for her and Reverend Bill to grow old together in. He didn't have much money as a preacher, but she worked enough to pay for everything, she'd explained. I saw this as a pure example of love. Mom was a good, dutiful wife; she didn't care that a man was living with his mom before she met him. Perhaps that was a lesson for me to stop nagging Reggie about money; after all, my mom didn't mind being the breadwinner. Plus, selfishly, Mom being in love and having something other than her poems to keep her warm at night made me feel less guilty that the only time we were guaranteed to see each other was Christmas, when both of us had time off from work. Just like her, I was committed to proving myself through a grueling work schedule that allowed little time for fun or family. That's what women like us have to do, she'd taught me. Work twice as hard to get half as far.

Christmas was my mom's favorite holiday. She always had Black Santas in the windows and scattered throughout her apartment. On my first Christmas visit home after the wedding, Reggie and I visited my mom and Reverend Bill's new row home. It had her usual plastic Santas but there also were new—and very alive—decorations: six caged pigeons in the dining room.

Those pigeons were cooing louder than the gospel music playing on my mom's kitchen radio. I knew they were Bill's pigeons, because, one, I would know if Mom started a damn bird-collecting hobby and two, Bill's divinity degree and the birds were the only items in the new house I didn't recognize from my mom's old apartment. From the Santas to the huge wood spoon and fork hanging in the kitchen, every other piece of decor was something my mom and I'd picked up while thrifting. The dining room pigeons were Bill's apparent sole marital contribution.

A small piece of white poo escaped one of the two cages and plopped down on my brother's graduation photo. As my mom shuffled over to wipe it off, I asked, "You going to introduce me to your flying roommates?" I figured it was a polite, nonconfrontational way to hint that eating Christmas dinner while watching pigeons shit was a tradition I did not want to become familiar with. My mom's eyes darted to the kitchen where Reverend Bill was on the phone. The birds had shat on my brother's photo, but they'd also apparently dropped eggshells because I could feel them under my feet as Mom walked me out of Bill's earshot. It was the first real sign that something wasn't quite right.

"Bill told me it doesn't make sense to pay for rental doves when we live so close to a pet store that sells white pigeons," she whispered. "The ones in the left cage are his funeral birds." That remark left me wondering why pigeons needed to be divided up by their jobs, but more so why she needed to whisper about it. I was glad I never loved a man enough to let him turn my dining room into an aviary. But I also knew that what I thought or felt didn't matter. My mom kept telling me she was happy, so I accepted it. More than just accepting it, I convinced myself that any bad vibes I got from Bill were my own issues.

That Christmas Eve, Jack, my younger brother, stopped by with his son, my nephew, Jay. After dinner we started our Christmas Eve tradition of each choosing one gift to open. My mom opened my Christmas card and fell into tears. I'm talking full-on sudden sobbing, like my Christmas card had punched her in the face.

I panicked. My brother and I exchanged nervous glances. *Our mom never cried. Over anything.* Reverend Bill stomped in from the kitchen, glaring at me.

"It's fine, I'm fine," Mom said as Reverend Bill grabbed her hand. She quickly reopened my Christmas card to show that she was stronger than whatever kryptonite it held. I relaxed. I figured once she'd read what I'd written in the card, she'd cheer up. I'd prepaid for what I thought was an amazing gift: outpatient surgery to get her right earlobe stitched up. Years ago, my mom's earlobe had split under the weight of her favorite hoop earrings and she'd resorted to wearing clips instead of having it repaired.

"Spending money on elective surgery for something that's not going to kill me? What am I, a Rothschild?" she'd ask whenever I'd suggest she get stitches. As thrift stores were both her furniture and jewelry stores of choice, our joyous holiday mother-daughter thrifting time had been replaced by the depressing realization that almost no one in Philadelphia wore clip earrings except my mom. So, yes, my gift was amazing because if time is money, then we'd spent billions in wasted shopping hours, but, more importantly, the gift would force my mom to accept something she considered a luxury. I had tried—and most often failed—to get her to let me spoil her. Mom found ways of refusing any gift that cost over $50. I wanted her to accept this small luxury, to know she deserved items that were a level above Applebee's.

"I can't use this gift," Mom said, lowering her head.

"You have to use it," I said, fully prepared to bat away her usual frugalness and excuses about how I should save all my money for myself. "And you better get used to being fussed over 'cause when I hit the real Hollywood big time, I'm going to buy you whatever car you want," I added. I then explained that just like you can't return a car once you drive it off the lot, I couldn't return that prepaid surgery. If there's one thing my mom hated more than spending too much money, it's wasting it entirely.

"So go on ahead and fix that fleshy wishbone-looking earlobe and wear your cute hoops," I said.

"Angela, stop. I already said I can't," she said, trying to get me to stop pushing. But I kept going.

"I already have a surgery scheduled," Mom added, frustrated. *There, happy now? You forced it out of me.*

You can't just cry and tell your daughter you're having surgery and expect her to continue opening her gift of socks, but my mom literally passed me socks in a Santa bag. She was done talking about her surgery.

I wasn't. I pressed her to explain what kind of surgery was serious enough to make you cry and prevent you from having two simple outpatient stitches. Bill maintained his glare on me, like questioning my own mother was rude.

"I'm getting a mastectomy," Mom said with a sigh. "I have breast cancer."

"Breast cancer?" my brother said, pushing himself up from the floor.

"It's fine. I'm fine," she said with a tight smile, waving his concern away. "The chemo and mastectomy will take care of everything."

My brother and I tried to press for more details, but Bill interjected.

"If your mom says she's fine, she's the nurse. Respect that and listen to her," he said.

So I did. I shut up and said nothing else. Because even if I could afford grown-up presents, I was still the child. Respecting her choices from birds to breast cancer surgery was more comfortable than a Christmas full of tears, tiptoeing over eggshells, and Bill's glare. My mom opened her other gifts, we ate, and a few days later my husband and I flew back to Los Angeles. Mom promised to tell me how the mastectomy went.

According to her, it went "fine."

———

At next year's Christmas visit, I tried to get more details about her health. My mom always danced around discussing it on the phone, insisting, as usual, that everything was fine. This Christmas, her home was decorated with the usual Black Santas, but pieces of new pink decor also competed with the birds and holiday theme. Bubblegum-hued ribbons and plaques dotted her walls and tables, each one shouting cursive commands like *Hope!* and *Have Strength!*

"The best thing you can do for your mom is keep her in your prayers," Bill said, answering for my mom as I asked for updates about her cancer. I stopped pushing and gave her another luxury gift, a mastectomy swimsuit and a first-class mother-daughter trip to Antigua. The gift was also for me: I wanted to get her alone, so I could ask about her health without Bill butting in.

"What am I going to do with this?" she asked, like it was a gag gift. "You know I can't swim." She laughed, but because that gift was also nonreturnable, Mom accepted it and while talking on the beach, away from Bill, I found the courage to interrupt the calm by asking more about her mastectomy.

I didn't expect her to say the cancer had returned in the other breast.

"But don't worry. After two mastectomies, the cancer won't have any more breasts to go to," she said, adding her signature chuckle. Her chuckle was real. Joyful. The same laugh she'd had when she'd started refusing overtime to go on dates with her now husband, so once again, I didn't push further. I listened to the waves crash against the shoreline and thought of all the signs that a double mastectomy was nothing to worry about. I found hope in remembering the overwhelming mastectomy swimsuit selection I'd seen online while picking out her gift; page after page of sexy photos of single and no-breasted women wearing bikinis and smiles while they swam and rode on Jet Skis. *Must be a lot of cancer-curing mastectomies or capitalism wouldn't make so many bikinis!* I held on to that thought so I didn't ruin our first mother-daughter trip by prying into the places my mom wanted to keep secret.

"Let's get that swimsuit wet!" I said as I ran into the water and motioned for my mom to join me, knowing her nonswimming self never would. She surprised me by walking in. Of course, she stopped once the water reached her shins, but that was deep enough that I had to take a photo. Whenever she took us to the Jersey Shore as kids, she ran from every wave like it was a possible tsunami. I couldn't believe I had finally convinced her to get in. I grabbed her disposable camera and she pointed proudly to the horizon then hauled ass back to the safety of our chairs.

"We should do this once a year," she said, still savoring her victory. The rest of the day, we sat on the sand and fantasized about where we'd travel next Christmas.

The following Christmas, all we'd done was fantasize because I was broke as shit. By that visit, I could no longer afford trips to Antigua and was barely affording my flight to Philly, courtesy of my recent divorce from Reggie and California laws about being the primary breadwinner in a joint-property state. This trip home, I was definitely not on the same page with my mom about being okay with a man only bringing birds to a marriage.

In addition to the divorce draining my pockets, my career was on life support. The already sporadic world of television sitcoms was nearly dead, taken over by cheaper-to-produce reality TV. I'd gone from being the first one to integrate the hit show *Scrubs*'s writing room to freelancing odd jobs and falling behind on my mortgage. I was ashamed. I couldn't hide the divorce from my mom but I damn sure was going to hide that my career had skipped past the "buy her whatever car she wants" stage and plunged down into the depths of praying daily that my own car would get stolen because I couldn't afford the payments. Mom was always so proud of how much I worked, she'd show off to her friends that my name was on TV. She'd find ways to casually sneak into conversations how I'd managed to move across the country and buy my own home. If I even hinted at having job troubles, Christmas would be ruined by my mom trying to catalog exactly what year she went wrong in how she raised me. To cover up my broke pockets, I went with a gift whose sentimentality would divert attention from how cheap it was: I'd won twenty pairs of clip earrings in a ninety-nine-cent online auction. I did not tell her that. I told her they were "imported" and "the kind you get in fancy LA shops."

"You notice anything different?" my mom asked as she tried a pair on, tilting her chin toward her chest as a hint.

"The scarf?" I asked. I was used to seeing her in hospital scrubs unless it was a Sunday. The button-down blouse and neck scarf were new. She told me she'd been promoted to management.

"I'm not on my feet as much. I even have my own desk and office," she said while fiddling with her scarf as if she wanted me to notice that specifically.

Bill once again interjected, giving me the answer my mom was fishing for: "She wants you to notice what's *not* under her scarf. Her breast. She got the other mastectomy. The cancer spread but the second mastectomy got it."

"Bill kisses my mastectomy scars and tells me I'm still beautiful," she said, motioning to where her breasts used to be and smiling like she was back in that moment, which made me internally gag. Mostly because "Mom having sex" makes most people's brains gag, but also because every Christmas, my present seemed to be hearing how great Bill was and getting shut out when I tried to ask questions.

"So the cancer's gone now?" I asked, trying to steer the conversation away from what she and Bill did in the bedroom.

"Yes. Praise God. Did I tell you Reverend Bill and I joined another church?" Mom asked, trying to change the subject to something more lighthearted.

It was their third church. They had a new one each Christmas I visited. My gut told me that was not normal. Still, I said nothing because a gut feeling is not proof, plus I suspected questioning any aspect of Bill would cause a wedge between my mom and me. We had no further talk of the double mastectomy, and that Christmas, we made plans for my mom and Bill to visit me in May.

May came. They didn't.

"Sorry, I can't come right now," Mom said, sounding as if her mind was focused on something other than the call. "I had to get some other little stuff done. Bill doesn't think I should fly."

"What other little stuff?" I asked, immediately worried. She'd never called me about her health.

"I need another round of chemo. Cancer just likes me, I guess," she said, and before I could comment, she added, "Thank god Bill likes me as much as cancer. That man takes such good care of me."

And while she went into detail yet again about how great Bill was, I shut up and listened as I usually did, but as soon as we hung up, I charged a next-day flight to Philadelphia, determined to kick through the wall Mom and Bill had erected around her diagnosis.

My brother shuffled around some work obligations to pick me up from the airport. Jack's son was in the back seat, and I had to swipe the front seat free of toys and picture books before I could sit. The kid brother who used to sneak forty ounces of beer with me now gave out hugs and bragged about his son tying his own sneakers. I hoped he'd retained just a bit of our teenage rebellion for this impromptu trip.

"You be good cop. I'mma be the bad cop and just tell Bill to shut the fuck up," my brother said, proving that despite driving a minivan, he still had the right amount of thug.

When we walked in on my mom, she was dressed in her new management blouse and scarf combo. *What form of cancer makes you unable to fly but still able to work?* I thought. We ordered in and, under the watchful eyes of now eight pigeons, listened to Reverend Bill say grace. After he thanked the Lord for the impromptu visit from his wife's daughter as well as the chicken cheesesteaks, he morphed the grace into a cancer update. He knew that was the reason for my sudden visit.

"And we thank you, God, for not having to worry about any new tumors that show up on Gwen," he said. "We don't worry about her masses, because we go to your mass—"

"Mom, you have a tumor?" I interrupted.

Bill cut me back off with more closed-eye prayer. I shot my brother and fellow heathen a look, knowing he'd have my back. Jack's eyes were indeed already open and he was biting his bottom lip. I could tell my brother was using every muscle in his mouth to keep it closed.

Bill finally tacked an amen onto his meandering grace. After sitting down, he turned to me. "Yes, there's a new mass," he said sharply. "But no matter what the doctors say, we know who has the ultimate chemo."

"Jesus," my mom answered.

Are they fucking serious?

"What'd you get on your cheesesteak, Bill? Provolone?" Mom asked, trying to maintain the facade of enjoying a meal and my surprise visit.

"No, we're not going to talk about cheese," my brother said, setting his bitten bottom lip free. "I want to know what's going on with the mass."

"I already told you—" Bill said.

"Yeah, *you* told us, but that's not who we're asking."

"I don't care who you're asking. I'm her husband—"

My brother didn't give a fuck who her husband was and told Bill exactly that. Bill jumped up from his chair. My brother did too.

"I will fuck you up. I don't care if you're a preacher."

Shit had just gotten real. I knew something was about to go down because my brother did not curse around our mom.

"Stop! Y'all scaring the pigeons!" I said, interrupting the men's shouting match. To be fair, the birds did look scared, but I knew two men nose to nose are not going to stop fighting because I love animals.

"Cut it out! My grandson is here," Mom said, giving a way better reason for them to stop fighting. She then calmly led my nephew away from the chaos to feed cheesesteak pieces to her two rescue Chihuahuas, Candi and Belle.

Bill and my brother kept shouting until it escalated into Bill lunging toward my brother. My brother shoved back, leaving Bill to thud against the wall before sliding down it, exactly as it happens in cartoons. Bill picked himself up, walked into the kitchen, and snatched open a drawer.

"He's getting a knife," I screamed, proving, just like with the birds, that I am utterly useless in a physical fight. I'm the chick yelling out commentary that no one needs. Plus, my commentary was wrong. Bill had, not a knife, but a hammer. Still, I dialed 911 as he crossed back into the dining room with the hammer above his head, aimed directly at my brother's skull. I screamed. My nephew screamed.

Upon hearing his son scream, my brother somehow suddenly became Thor and dead-stopped the hammer in midair. With his free hand, he shoved Reverend Bill into the hall closet. I was standing in a daze. *How did my surprise visit turn into this?*

Then Mom threw a bucket of water at me.

"Sorry, I meant that for Bill and Jack," she said, explaining to a thoroughly drenched me that she'd learned in nursing school to break up fights with water. She handed me a towel, then turned to her grandson, Jay, a huge grin on her face.

"Isn't this fun? We're having an indoor water fight!" she exclaimed to Jay, then explained the adults were only screaming because we were so excited about the one day each year we get to make puddles inside the house! We all followed Mom's lead and pretended mopping was also a game as my brother wedged himself against the closet door, keeping Reverend Bill trapped inside until the police arrived.

2

Psalm 23 and Stage 4

'm so sorry about this. I have cancer, it's been hard for him," my mom explained to the cops as they handcuffed Bill. After he was placed in the police car, she then gave the same "it's the stress of my cancer" apology to the neighbors who had gathered on their porches to figure out why so many cops were on their quiet block.

I flinched when she used her illness to explain away Bill's actions. Every time she apologized, I wanted to scream, but over the years, I'd learned to begrudgingly accept that my mom prided herself on being polite to a fault. She'd literally yell "sorry" to a phone for not getting to its ring quickly enough. Of course, she was going to apologize to her neighbors for the commotion. She also apologized to them several times for my shirt being so drenched that they could see my bra through it.

Well, I guess now ain't a bad time to bring up the cancer. Can't ruin the visit any more than it has been already. After her West Philly apology tour, she and I sat alone in the living room. I planned to ask about the new mass we'd prayed about after I broke the silence with a joke. When I kept it PG, I could always make my mom laugh, even when we were as exhausted as we were that night. I had the perfect joke in my head. I was going to ask her why Reverend Bill grabbed a hammer instead of a knife. *Was he planning on crucifying my brother? Was that more biblically acceptable than a regular ol' stabbing?*

I didn't get a chance to say my joke; Mom kicked off the cancer conversation herself simply by unwrapping her work scarf from her neck. Scarf unwrapped, I saw hard lima bean–size lumps covering almost every inch of the usual smooth brown skin on her neck. Removing her scarf was, perhaps, an inadvertent act, but it was one that freed her neck to tell me secrets her mouth never could. Those angry lumps refused to go along with her plans to conceal how bad her cancer had gotten.

"Those are my lymph nodes," she said matter-of-factly.

I nodded back as if I understood, but I didn't. I barely knew what lymph nodes did. I didn't even understand how breast cancer could spread. She'd told me after the double mastectomy the cancer would have no place to go. Why did we label a cancer with one body part if it could spread wherever it wanted? Why didn't we call it "Breast Cancer FOR NOW, if you're lucky?" My mom, who always insisted she was "fine, just fine," was finally admitting that she wasn't and I had only ignorance to offer in return.

"Look at what they put in my chest," she said, unbuttoning the top three buttons on her blouse. "Aftermarket parts," she said, holding my gaze as I looked over what she'd revealed: Just inches down from her neck, a short tube had been surgically implanted in the middle of her chest, between the scars where her breasts used to be.

"I'm— I'm at stage 4 now. I'm dying, Angela."

I didn't have ignorance to offer then. I knew exactly what to say.

"No, you're not!"

I said it with all the indignation she'd used on me when, as a teen, I dared to ask for something she forbid. The explicit version of a rap cassette. To attend a party with no parents. To wear a tank top that showed too much tit. I didn't ask her why she thought she was dying. I just absolutely knew I was not going to allow it. I was pissed she'd even said the *d*-word. *How dare she use that word around me!* I had to let her know that she raised a better daughter than one who would sit idly by and listen to her talk about her own death. I invoked the words of her God.

"You always said he doesn't give us more than we can handle," I said.

I reminded her of her age, like she'd somehow forgotten.

"You're only sixty-four. No one in our family dies that young!"

I used her own pink decor against her.

"What do your kitchen magnets say? They say 'Have Strength! Hope! Perseverance!'"

My admonishment seemed to push her little "dying thing" back a bit. She went silent. Of course, maybe she went silent because you're not supposed to admonish your mother and shut her down with kitchen magnet slogans when she's finally opening up about her cancer. Yes, perhaps that was a bit much after a day already filled with police and pretend water fights. Still, I was certain she wasn't dying. Dying people don't casually announce their deaths while sitting in their work clothes, picking at a reheated chicken cheesesteak.

———

The next morning, I texted my brother.

> **Me:** Mom thinks she's dying!!
> **Jack:** What the fuck?
> **Me:** She never said that to u?
> **Jack:** Like I wouldn't hv called u if she had! It's the stress of
> Reverend Bill and the arrest making her say that.

When Mom woke up from her overnight sleep on the couch, she confirmed my brother's suspicion.

"Who called the cops on Reverend Bill?"

"Me," I replied.

She frowned.

"Sorry, next time someone tries to hammer my brother, I'll just turn the other cheek. My bad," I said, despite knowing that my sarcasm wasn't one of Mom's favorite things.

"I have an oncologist appointment on Monday! Who is going to take me if Bill is in jail?"

"I think the better question is, why are you going to the oncologist if you're supposedly dying?" I said, certain I had caught her in a Sherlock Holmes *Aha!* moment.

She explained that she was getting a PICC (peripherally inserted central catheter) line. I took that as another point on my "mom not dying" scoreboard. As with lymph nodes, I barely knew what a PICC line was for. My big brain just knew that people who are dying don't need lines of any kind.

Mom continued worrying about getting to her appointment because, as she told me, Bill chauffeurs her everywhere, even to work every day. She motioned to an overstuffed binder under the coffee table.

"Can you grab that for me? It has the doctor's number so I can call to cancel the appointment."

"Nope. You're not canceling it. I'll take you to your appointment so I can understand what the hell is going on," I said, nervous that I was now piling commands on top of my sarcasm.

As expected, she argued. Insisted I fly back home to my life. She still didn't know I didn't have much of a life left—or at least the parts we both considered successful. I countered that if I was flying home, she was coming with me. I wasn't leaving her alone in a house where I noticed she could barely walk up the stairs. She shut down. She didn't need my help.

"I said no," Mom said, an edge to her voice that let me know that she was still the parent.

"Well, I'm not leaving. I'll just move in," I said, sinking into her sofa defiantly.

⸻

Bill's arrest made me resolute to finally become the superhero I'd always aspired to be: *Mom Hoarder Extraordinaire.*

Since I can remember I loved having my mom to myself. I stayed in her stomach for an extra two weeks and even after the obstetrician forced me out, I dedicated my early childhood to trying to keep her close. I loved her silliness. To wake me up in the morning, she'd play albums on my plastic Fisher-Price record player and pretend to scratch them like a hip-hop deejay. She jumped double Dutch and she could make every cartoon voice from Disney. When she brought Jack home from the hospital, she started sharing her silliness with him and four-year-old me knew I had no choice but to try to kill him.

"Can I push him?" I apparently asked after my mom placed newborn Jack into a baby swing. "Of course," my mom said, proud that I was stepping into the older sister role so easily. BLAM! I double-handedly shoved the shit out of that swing and Jack would have tumbled right into our '70s-style sunken living room if not for my mom's swift reflexes.

When my mom made the unsmooth transition to divorced, single mom, I had to not only share her with my younger brother, but with these two new bitches: Overtime and Double Overtime. Those bitches had always been hovering around, helping our family with Grown Folks Problems, but once my mom became a single parent, they rang our house every night. My mom always happily answered their calls and I didn't understand why those needy heffas had become so important to her. Hoarding a sliver of my mom's free time became something young me could only manage on rare weekends when Overtime didn't call. On one of those weekends, my mother casually invited our neighbors over. They brought their daughter, Destiny.

Now, I usually dug Destiny. She was cool. She played a good game of Red Light, Green Light and what have you. But that day, Destiny was cutting into my Mom Hoard Time. The straw that broke my preadolescent back was when I took a pee break from playing with Destiny. As my little legs dangled off the toilet seat, I heard my mom doing her Donald Duck impression for Destiny. It was bad enough my mom shared it with my brother, but sharing it with someone other than blood? That could not stand.

"Do it again," Destiny pleaded. As my mom did, I leaped off the toilet seat and snapped. I couldn't push Destiny out of a swing, but I could use a weapon I'd learned was just as painful. Words.

"Destiny bites people, Mom!" I yelled, while pulling up my pants and dashing out to save my mom from Destiny's front teeth. "Don't do Donald Duck for her! She'll bite you!"

My mom stopped me middash. "Apologize! Now!"

I got sent to my room, losing out on even more mom time.

As I aged into my preteen years, the babysitters who filled in for my mom switched from pleading with me to leave my mom be to lecturing me on how being almost grown meant learning to be without her.

"Other people don't see their moms because of men or drugs. She's only gone because she goes to work to take care of you." She was the tough superhero single mom, a woman who could be both parents as well as the breadwinner and never let her kids see her sweat. Adults often told me that when I was older I'd understand that I was lucky to have a mom who knew the value of working twice as hard.

I never felt lucky, but as I grew up and tried to not be so needy, I started to see the world as she saw it, that working twice as hard was a given. That you never complained about it, instead you kept your head down and struggled as hard as you could in a world that was often cruel to women on their own. Anything else was giving up. Instead of constantly being under my mom, my adult life became dedicated to making her proud by working as hard as she did, even if it meant I only saw her on Christmas. After she told me she was dying, I decided I'd only channel my hard work into making sure she understood that dying was giving up. And like she'd taught me, giving up was something women like us don't have the luxury to do.

3

Nebuchadnezzar and Know-It-Alls

Jack and I deduced that we had two days to plot out a new Bill-free cancer care plan for Mom. We didn't deduce that on our own; we'd called a childhood friend who had a state-issued ankle bracelet and knew about the inner workings of the court system. He told us Bill would be locked up for the weekend.

"Getting locked up on Friday is the worst. He won't be out until Monday when he can see a judge," he said before also suggesting my brother get a protection order against Reverend Bill.

"That's what I got against my wife," our friend advised, telling us more than we needed to know about his marriage.

⁓

Day One. When Mom awoke on Saturday, I tried to win her over by feigning excitement at being able to attend church with her the next day. Usually, I scheduled my trips home to avoid Sundays. This time, I bounced right up to her like the Holy Ghost had saved me in my sleep.

"I'm not going to church," my mom replied. She had to know that announcement was almost as big of a bombshell as announcing she was dying. The last time she'd skipped church was because her car literally broke down. I was thirteen and I remember feeling cool as hell that I was in charge of the steering wheel while she pushed the car to the side of the road. This time her reason for skipping church wasn't because she'd bought a $500 car with a salvage title.

"I don't have a church to go to. Reverend Bill isn't a real reverend," she said, pointing to Bill's always multiplying divinity degrees. Her voice was hushed and timid, like she was trusting me with gossip she'd been forbidden to share. She explained that his degrees weren't worth the paper they were printed on. They were always switching churches because someone in the clergy always eventually found out that anyone with a pulse and tuition money could possess the same degrees that graced my mom's dining room.

"I drained my retirement to get him those degrees," Mom said and lowered her head as she explained the embarrassment of going from preacher's wife with a premium parking space to not having a church home at all. Each time they were kicked out of a church, Bill promised her it was a misunderstanding and asked her to pay for a new school, one he'd absolutely, positively thoroughly researched this time. She always trusted him. She always gave him more money, and still, the schools were always bogus and they continually had to change churches, she explained while bracing for my judgment. It hurt that she felt I would judge her. *My mom doesn't know me at all as an adult*, I thought. That was something else I'd fix that weekend.

"I know you're not apologizing for a bad choice in men?" I asked, using my entire dating history and recent divorce to soothe her shame. My divorce was something my mom wasn't exactly proud of; she'd asked me not to tell her church friends. Now, it had become something to bond over; something to show her that I could deal with her bad marriage news and anything else she threw my way. I had emerged from my divorce highly skilled in fixing relationship mistakes, at least monetary ones.

"Bill still on your bank accounts?" I asked.

I told her to get dressed. We were driving to her banks so he couldn't drain whatever money he hadn't already drained.

"Let's take his SUV," she said excitedly as if we were two crime bosses planning a getaway mission. I was pleasantly surprised she agreed to follow my lead so easily, but even more surprised that her broke-ass husband had an SUV.

"His SUV?" I asked.

"I bought it for him. He said it was more comfortable to drive me to work in," she said, shrugging, before casually adding that she'd taken out a five-figure loan to cover the cost. I refrained from asking in what world a five-foot-four man needed "more leg room" as we drove to her bank to withdraw all the cash she hadn't spent on Bill. She had less than $1,500 after forty-four years of nonstop work.

We took that cash and opened a new account at a bank I knew had branches in Los Angeles. Although I didn't tell her, I knew part of her new cancer care plan would be convincing her to move across the country with me. I knew this would be no easy feat. Mom was born in West Philadelphia and never lived more than one neighborhood away from her parents. She worked for the same Philadelphia hospital for over forty years. She thrived on stability and routine. If something was too far from home, she didn't need it. As a child, the farthest I remember her driving was Delaware. She only ventured that far after learning Delaware had no sales tax and that by braving a toll road she could save money on school clothes. She always made a big deal out of pointing to the Welcome to Delaware sign. It was her Rushmore. Crossing a single state line was my mother's version of a Great American Road Trip.

When I'd told Mom I was moving to Los Angeles, she reacted as if I told her I was planning to colonize Mars. She warned me that California was a land of unreligious weirdos who chased dreams, and when their dreams collapsed, they shot up heroin and robbed people like me. It was not a place for a woman to live alone. She worried about everything from gangs to new bills that passed the California Senate floor. She called to make sure I hadn't lost everything in wildfires that were several California counties away. She made me promise that I'd return to the safety of Philadelphia when my completely landlocked home washed away because "some person" on "some news program" said California was falling into the ocean. To Mom, moving to California meant running away from stability to a place where even the ground shook underneath your feet.

Still, she needed so much she wasn't getting—a bedroom she could reach without stairs, rest from work, and most importantly, shiny, celebrity Hollywood doctors who knew about treatment and cures that plebian Philadelphia doctors didn't. I knew if she came to California, she wouldn't die. I knew that in Hollywood, there are doctors who risk their licenses to give actors any pills they desire. I was sure I could find one MD who knew what pills to prescribe to stave off something as ubiquitous as cancer. I tried to figure out how to force her to make one more hard choice in what had been years of choices that had done nothing for her—from trusting her own husband to rounds of chemo to double mastectomies.

As Saturday's sun set, I dipped my toe back into the topic of her moving, afraid that Bill would call and spit a Bible verse that would scare her into reconciling with him. I soft-launched the idea of her finding a new place to live so that she wouldn't have to live with Bill when he was released.

"I'd like to know how he's going to be released with no money. I'm not paying his bond. He already called and asked," she said, ending her sentence with a laugh so loud, the pigeons flinched. I laughed with her, then had to tell her—she who had never even gotten a speeding ticket—that there were things criminals could get called bail bonds by putting up their home equity.

"Well, he's not on the house. I might have been a fool for him but I'm no fool," she countered, her pride kicking in and letting me know that she wasn't so stupid she needed me for every damn thing. She was, in fact, the one who told me to make sure the marital house I'd paid for was only in my name, a lesson she'd learned after losing our childhood home to my father.

"Bill better call one of his other women to get him out of the clink," she continued. "Yep, his old behind used the word *clink* when he called me," Mom said, again falling into laughter.

"The clink! Those dirty *coppers*!" I said.

"You called the *fuzz* on him!" she said, and after a few minutes, we ran out of old-timey slang, and I got up the nerve to ask her about Bill's other dames and broads.

"Yeah," my mom said, suddenly deflated again, "I think it's a few women from church. I pay for our family phone plan and he doesn't know I can see every number he calls." She laughed yet again. By then, I'd grown tired of her gentle nature. Her apologies. Her laughs to cover up her pain. I wanted her to be mad. Mad enough to move in with me.

"This is a lot. I really think you should move to California," I dared to suggest. She gave her biggest laugh of all in response to that, like the thought of moving was crazier than marrying a cheating fake preacher who used outdated slang.

"I have $1,500 to my name. I have cancer. I need to work to keep my health insurance. I can't just take a vacation to California."

I stopped pressing. I could figure out how to fight those other concerns while she slept. I hoped while she slept her resting brain was absorbing how much of an adult I'd become since I'd moved across the country, how much I understood, and, perhaps more importantly, how much I wasn't afraid of learning. As she snored on the couch, I made a midnight coffee and took the overstuffed cancer binder to the kitchen table and started reading.

The papers in the binder were in no particular order, like a junk drawer of three years of oncologist visits. I desperately tried to cram my way through the pages like I was back in school, when bringing home an A was all I needed to get my book-smart mom's praise and hoard an extra moment of her love and free time. I'm not saying I started off that midnight study session thinking I could find a cure—I mean, I'm no scientist—but I am admitting that I thought because I loved her more than her doctors did that I could, at least, spot something they had missed. Okay, and, perhaps, as a side effect of that, I could at least cure her specific cancer—the breast kind. The kind that her pink decor was so upbeat about.

That Saturday night, I did not cure cancer. Not her cancer nor any other cancer. I did, in fact, spend a lot of moments hating on every pink piece of decor that ordered her to persevere and hope. From the little I could understand from her binder, cancer was a rapidly multiplying monster intent on destroying every part of my mom's body. It was not pink. Pink monsters are usually ones you can trust to save you from the other ones. After online-searching complex medical words that seemed like gibberish, only to be led to more words that sounded like someone threw consonants against the wall just to frustrate me, I gave up. I decided to go to sleep and get ready for a weekend day where I'd have my mom all to myself. The kind of day I'd wanted ever since Destiny's vampire teeth got me sent to my room.

Day Two. On Sunday, when I awoke and went downstairs, my mom was dressed in a blouse and in the middle of tidying up.

"Really? You're going to work?" I asked, ready to tackle her if she tried to open the front door.

"No, I get my pleural catheter drained today. Crystal, the lady who does it, should be here soon." She pointed to the tube under her blouse.

"You don't need to point! I know that tube is called a pleural catheter," I admonished her, leaving off that I'd just looked it up during my cancer cram session last night. I had googled both "pleural" and "catheter" because I had absolutely no idea that catheters drained things other than penises and vaginas.

I desperately wanted Crystal to like me. Anyone who came into my mom's house was going to be an instrument in my plan to get her on a plane to LA.

"How can we get Reverend Bill to learn to do this, Miss Gwen?" Crystal asked, while taking off her jacket and setting down a bag of medical supplies. Crystal's medical bag was the size of a kid's lunch box. From it, she unpacked a plastic bottle attached to a spaghetti-thin drainage line. "You over here trying to spend time with your daughter and here I come holding you up," Crystal continued, talking to my mom with the ease of a woman who had learned to make playful small talk to distract from the pain of pleural catheters.

My mom made excuses for Bill, yet again. "The only reason he won't do it is because he's scared of hurting me."

"He doesn't need to be scared! He's seen me do it, it's not hard," Crystal continued.

"Well, you know how some men are . . ." my mom said, her voice trailing off.

Crystal turned to me. "You wanna learn?"

"Yes, ma'am! I was just reading about it last night," I said, then jumped up like an overlooked bench player prepared to deliver a touchdown for Coach Crystal.

Perhaps Crystal should have picked up that I was a bit overeager. That I was trying my damnedest to telepath to my mom: *Did you notice I, an adult, offered to drain your lungs, something Bill wouldn't do! Did you also notice this draining device fits in a carry-on bag that we can pack for California?*

"Your mom's not going to be able to talk while we do this, so I'm going to use the time to ask you Hollywood gossip," Crystal said, laughing.

Oh, Crystal, you're the gift that keeps on giving. Of course, my mom had not introduced me simply as her daughter but her "successful daughter" who "lives in Los Angeles and writes for TV." I usually hated when she did this. Her lavish introductions usually resulted in someone pitching me why their workplace should be a show and my mom forcing me to meet with them for coffee because "you never know, NBC could be looking for a sitcom about the braiding salon." If they didn't pitch me a show, they'd, like Crystal, often want gossip about the celebrities I worked with. I'd always lie and tell Mom's friends that celebrities are exactly the fun, genuine people they seem to be in the scripts and awards speeches we write for them. There was a celebrity who threw a script across the writers' room so hard it left a paper cut under my eye. I told people in Philadelphia that celebrity was "a force" and that "I appreciated that she kept me on my feet." With Crystal, I found myself enjoying remixing tales of celebrity cruelty into positive spin. I wanted Crystal and my mom to think Los Angeles was the promised land, especially for their demographic: underpaid women in health care.

"In Hollywood, rich people overpay for everything! They don't just have nannies, they hire full-time nurses. I know a nurse's aide who makes more than some Philly doctors!" I said, forcing my mute mom to listen to Crystal beg to be in her spot.

"Ooh, Mom, you going to Hollywood?" Crystal asked. "If you don't I will!" My mom rolled her eyes. *Here we go again.*

"She's worried about money. About finding a job," I said. "If she only knew what I knew from being out there. She doesn't even have to be a nurse if she doesn't want to. We can open a thrift store." I kept talking, trying to tap into how every single time my mom and I shopped together looking for those damn clip earrings, we'd day-dream aloud about opening our own thrift shop where she could set aside every donated clip earring for herself.

"We'll call our store Our Little Boutique. Right, Mom?" I asked, knowing she could only answer with her eyes. She again rolled them.

Time on my side, I kept going about Our Little Boutique. I always thought the name was too generic, but my mom insisted on our pretend store having that name. "Our Little Boutique" was our mother-daughter code phrase for secondhand store. If some-one complimented my mom on an outfit, I could tell how close they were by whether she answered "this thrift store in the hood where everything is a dollar" (truth) or "some little boutique" (lit-tle white lie).

"Seriously, if she comes to California and opens a thrift store, she'll be rich. Look up what a vintage bootleg LL Cool J T-shirt goes for out there."

Crystal searched her laptop and found the answer. "You have got to be kidding me!" she exclaimed, showing my mother that a "Ladies Love Cool James" shirt we could easily find at our hood thrift was featured on a collectibles website.

The pleural tube still draining, I jabber-jawed my way through more uninterrupted pitching: "I also figured out a new big money hustle. Civil War coins." I was 100 percent serious about my mom and I being coin hunters. With no current income, I'd quickly dove back into finding new ways to almost make ends meet. I'd transitioned from a strictly Lego phase (who knew they sold for so much?) to using a metal detector to search for coins. I was doing horribly at it because, one, I was self-conscious carrying it around the park and, two, because it was a shitty basic model someone apparently donated to the thrift store because it could only detect pennies and screws. But perhaps the biggest reason I sucked at metal detecting was that I lived in California where there was no Civil War. People near Philly, though? I'd read in my online forums how they'd found coins that sold for up to $5,000 each.

"You think L.L. tees are worth a lot, wait until you look up how much an 1865 nickel goes for," I told Crystal as I noticed the fluid draining from my mom's lungs had slowed to an intermittent drip. It was like a liquid hourglass telling me I was running out of time to sell my California dreams.

"Also, I can load up a car with Philadelphia bricks, drive them across the country and sell them for five figures," I said, explaining that I'd once attended a swanky outdoor party at a hilltop Malibu mansion and after the usual cocktail party small talk, I'd complimented the host's wide, bricked driveway. It's rare to see homes with brick features in Los Angeles; bricks and earthquakes don't get along. The party host remembered I was from Philadelphia and proudly explained that the driveway we were standing on was made from "real Philadelphia colonial antique reclaimed bricks" that cost more than his swimming pool. As soon as I ditched that party, my broke ass went home and looked up how much Philadelphia historic bricks sell for and tucked that information away into a brain file called Dumb Shit I Can Easily Acquire That Rich People Buy.

Every brick house in Philly was technically historic. My mom and I could excavate the hood and become instant millionaires.

"The bricks are easy money. And yet here we are using one for a doorstop," I said, motioning to the actual red brick my mom used to prop her basement door open. Mom shook her head at me. She looked pissed that I was recruiting Crystal into my California move cult. Thank goodness she didn't ask me how I suddenly knew so much about making a living through other people's trash.

Crystal started taking notes. I told her to add my cell number to her notes.

"You can come visit us anytime. I have a spare bedroom," I said, not adding that that room would hopefully be my mom's so Crystal would have to crash at the motel down the street.

My mom coughed, a side effect of draining the pleural catheter. Crystal motioned for me to stop draining.

"It's important to not try to drain every single drop. Her lungs can only handle so much."

"You should be more like your lungs, Mom," I said, getting in one last uninterrupted quip.

After Crystal left, my mom caught her breath. "I see . . . what you're trying to do. You're not slick. We'll ask—" she said, before pausing to cough again. "We'll ask the doctor . . . what he thinks tomorrow about California."

It wasn't much, but I took it as a win. A real win would have been her agreeing we had time to make up for. That she also dreamed of leaving it all behind to open a thrift store with me. I wanted her to tell me that I was the best daughter she could have ever had and of course she trusted me to save her life. I wanted her to throw caution to the wind and jet out of town with me on some Thelma and Louise shit. She flew to Vegas to marry Bill. Why couldn't I get that same spontaneity? I knew the answer. Trusting a man of God was a safer choice than trusting me. Men of God at least had prayers for her pain. What did I have? I'd just learned that breast cancer could spread beyond breasts and acted like I deserved a Nobel Prize for draining one catheter. I knew I had to show Mom that I may not have as much God on my side as Reverend Bill pretended to have, but I definitely still had enough book smarts. I decided to change course and show her it was safe to move because I could become as much of an expert on her cancer as her doctor. I was determined to study up and win her oncologist over just as I'd done with Crystal. Plus, how hard could it be to impress a doctor who was letting his patient die? What part of the Hippocratic Oath was that?

4

Foam Slippers and Other Sins We Don't Talk About

feared that if I slipped up once before her appointment, my mom would claim amnesia before asking her doctor a damn thing about moving. There was a chance that if I stuttered on one medical word, she would remember that I was the same child who wanted to drop out of high school to become a rapper. M.C. Angela was not equipped to be a cancer caretaker. I imagined winning her oncologist over, only to have Mom loudly announce that I didn't know how to pronounce *esophagogastroduodenoscopy* or *dimethylamidophenyldimethylpyrazolone*. Yes, those are real-ass words. Someone was clearly showing off when they came up with them. No words need to be that long.

I started stepping up my medical smarts game, determined to show my mom I was not only an adult in the way I deftly removed fluid from her chest, but I was also an adult who could talk confidently, knowledgeably, to the doctor about the medical reason I was removing the fluid. Before Mom's oncology appointment, I jumped back into that coffee table cancer binder to soak up as much knowledge as I could.

I had nicknamed the cancer binder "the BCB" because that shorthand was more manageable to text my brother than "big cancer binder." Plus, typing the word *cancer* over and over was depressing. *Fuck cancer*, right? It doesn't even deserve to be called by its government name. My brother and I ping-ponged texts back and forth trying to unravel the mystery words and courses of treatment I found inside the BCB.

> **Me:** She didn't tell us she had two rounds of radiation. Is that the same as chemo?
>
> **Me:** The BCB says she sees a physical therapist. Why are you seeing a physical therapist if you're dying? Aren't they for athletes?
>
> **Me:** I just found two fast-food receipts in the BCB. I know those are Bill's. Always talking about he has "the gout" but drinking McDonald's sodas. I hope he falls down the subway steps WHICH HE IS NOW TAKING BECAUSE I HAVE THE KEYS TO HIS STUPID SUV.

That night, as I again flipped open the crammed BCB, despite my newfound cancer moxie, I couldn't get through a half page before stumbling over lines that seemed to be written in code. What the hell is "ER+(weakly) /PR-, HER2-. Diffuse adenopathy"? What does it mean that "A transthoracic right upper lobe ultrasound-guided core fine needle aspiration was negative for acid fast bacilli by fluorochrome stain"? I decided to accept that I was dumb as shit and my liberal arts degree was, indeed, worthless in the real world. On one of the pages, I saw my mom's spiky cursive; underneath a reminder to "Get greens for Sunday," she'd written "Triple Negative." On Google's first page of results was something my brain could finally understand: Black women were more likely to have triple-negative breast cancer.

That can't be good.

"When white America has a cold, Black America has the flu," was one of the sayings Mom would always use to explain American inequality. Coming of age during Jim Crow, she not only had sayings, she had concrete experience in how afflictions affecting white Americans affected Black Americans twice as much. From reading the search results, my mom did seem to have the flu of cancers. I learned that triple negative is more deadly than other cancers. It comes back more often and spreads more violently. Science had only discovered triple-negative breast cancer five years before my mom was diagnosed. One cancer fact I did know from my liberal arts degree was that cancer was discovered in 3000 BC. (Thank you, anthropology!) How did no one notice for five thousand years that a different, more aggressive type of cancer was affecting Black women? Were those nonprofit pink donations my mom had made even funding research for her type of breast cancer?

In the spirit of staying positive and using the internet as the echo chamber it was designed to be, I searched the more general "Stage 4 breast cancer survival rates" to run away from the dismal triple-negative prognosis. The five-year survival rate for general all-kinds of breast cancer was around 30 percent. That statistic wasn't unbridled positivity, but it was more positivity than was found under the "triple-negative" search. If someone told me I'd have a 30 percent chance at winning the lottery, I'd play my ass off. I didn't dig deeper in the search to see the exact percentage of survivors who were triple negative. I didn't add "for Black women" to the search. I didn't want to find the flu. I did, however, find a long-abandoned blog from a woman who claimed to have survived and cured her stage 4 breast cancer with items purchased at health food stores.

Unlike the BCB, I understood every word in that blog. Well, the parts that I actually read. The author had written long, heartfelt entries detailing her cancer struggle and I skipped right over to those to get to her remedy list. Then I cross-checked her remedy list with holistic doctors' opinions and in about twenty minutes, I was convinced that I didn't need to learn big words; I could reverse my mom's cancer with a new diet, mass market vitamins, and something called orgonite. This may sound like an insane way to impress my book-education-loving mom into believing I could care for her, but it's not. I knew the straight line she followed from church to work curved just a bit when it came to trusting the science of the work she did. Working in health care, she was keenly aware that the peer-reviewed science often didn't include her peers. She was alive when Henrietta Lacks "unknowingly" donated her cells; she'd also taught my brother and me about the Tuskegee experiment and Dr. James Marion Sims.

"The more things change, the more they stay the same. Some of these doctors still don't treat patients equally," she'd often say on our catch-up calls. That was one of the reasons Mom worked so much. To fight for patients who didn't even know what they were allowed to fight for. And that's what I was doing for her by driving to Whole Foods to purchase everything mentioned in that blog. At the very least, store-bought vitamins don't have a history of systemic racism and sexism.

"What is all this?" my mom asked, peering cautiously into one of my shopping bags, like the contents might make her cry just like my shitty Christmas card.

I explained what I'd found on the blog. And then explained that, of course, I wasn't insane and relying only on the blog. I'd done further research and also found other natural, organic anti-cancer treatment protocols recommended by top doctors.

"Dr. Reich put live cancer cells next to shaved orgonite and every cancerous cell died," I explained.

"What kind of doctor was he?" Mom asked.

"A medical one," I said, hoping that my confidence concealed how lame that answer was. I didn't have time to search to see exactly what type of doctor he was. Even if he was a damn chiropractor, if he had a hint on how to cure cancer with the electrical powers of orgonite, we were going to try it.

My mom put on her reading glasses and peered at one of the vitamin bottles. "I guess we can ask Dr. Fox if these are okay," she said, then turned away from the vitamins and turned on the kitchen radio. Behind me, a choir sang that things aren't over until God says they are: I simply had to give God the opportunity to work a miracle. And I was. I ordered two shaved orgonite spheres online.

At her oncologist's office, while a nursing assistant weighed my mom, I reviewed my notebook, which held the weekend's unanswered "super book smart daughter" questions. I wanted Dr. Fox to know I'd done my research, that I wasn't just jumping into the cancer caretaker pool without knowing how to at least doggie-paddle. I was going for deferential yet competent. I wanted Dr. Fox to understand that I knew he was in charge . . . until I could sign my mom up with a Hollywood oncologist who would tell us how wrong and antiquated Dr. Fox's Philadelphia treatments were.

"This is my daughter, she writes for medical shows," my mom said, perhaps warning him that I was a know-it-all or just doing her usual showing off about the career she didn't know no longer existed. I wondered if she'd forgotten that I'd met Dr. Fox once before. Bill was also there. I'd spent a good part of my time in Dr. Fox's office trying to crawl inside myself after Reverend Bill interrupted the doctor to lead us all in prayer. I remember Dr. Fox awkwardly putting down his clipboard to clasp my hand for what I assume was his first-ever Black prayer circle. I remembered his hands being softer than I imagined a middle-aged doctor's to be. If Dr. Fox remembered me or noticed that the man who had led that prayer circle was missing, he didn't let on. He was kind, but all business, preparing to place a PICC line for more chemo.

"Hopefully, the fifth round will be the charm," he said.

Before I snooped around in the BCB, I only knew of one round. I'd flown home for Mom's first outpatient treatment, not knowing that one round of chemo has many cycles. I thought a round was like the ones at bars, one round at a time. Who knew a round contained many cycles? Probably every single person but me. Still, I propose a rule that if a word has multiple meanings, we start learning all meanings at the same time.

In addition to learning how the four rounds of chemo didn't help, I learned that neither did the radiation, nor a clinical drug trial. I went from trying to impress Dr. Fox with multisyllabic words to feeling dumb as hell. I couldn't have that, so I switched gears and tried to put Dr. Fox on the defensive.

"So, she's gone through every treatment you suggested with no improvement. Is there any reason to actually think more chemo would work?" I asked, hoping my question didn't come off as distrust or, even worse, solidify that I was the most medically ignorant person to ever enter an oncologist's office with her mom. Maybe five rounds was, indeed, the magic number.

Dr. Fox explained that not all chemo treatments were the same and that there are different cocktails. As he explained the potential possibilities, I noticed the comfort my mom had with Dr. Fox seemed to slowly dissolve. The more he talked about chemo, the more my mom seemed to get smaller. I wondered if she was reliving the brutality of the things he'd called potential cures.

Seeing her shrink, I dove into my notebook and asked the one question that wasn't written to make me sound smart.

"What you would do if she was your mom?" I asked. That was the question that mattered. I wanted him to see my mom not as a patient, but as someone I desperately needed to have around for decades more.

Dr. Fox paused before answering. "If it were my mom, I wouldn't do more chemo," he said, almost apologetically. "But, the choice is up to you, Gwen."

Of course the choice was up to her, but did he have to tell her that? I mean, ethically he probably did, but we'd just established she'd had a strong history of saying yes to as many treatments as he proposed.

"Angela wants me to go stay with her in California," my mom said, changing the subject. "If I leave, people are going to say, 'How can Gwen take a vacation to Hollywood but she can't come into work?!'" Her voice had a sudden franticness; she feared people's judgment more than additional rounds of chemo.

"A vacation? Who is going to say that? You have cancer," I said. My god, even with stage 4 cancer, my mom's job was trying to take her away from me.

"Yeah, I don't think anyone will say you're on a vacation," Dr. Fox said, confused. He stole a look my way as if understanding that, like me, he was suddenly getting a glimpse into secret parts of my mom. The doctor and I were even: I was dumb on her medical, he was dumb on her emotional. I shot him a look that said, *See what I'm dealing with here? Help me.*

"Go with your daughter," Dr. Fox said. I appreciated how he phrased it. Like an order. To my mom, if the educated doctor at the Ivy League hospital orders you to go with your daughter, that's what you do. Just like getting a PICC line.

"If you'd like, I can arrange for chemo in California," Dr. Fox added.

"I-I don't want to do it again," my mom replied softly, almost as if she was asking his permission to not put herself through the agony.

"Don't apologize. Chemo is brutal," Dr. Fox said, and I was prepared to book my mom's flight to Los Angeles that second. Having won him over, I held out my arm to help my mom get up from her seat. She let my helping hand hang in midair as she turned back to Dr. Fox.

"Have you ever heard of a Dr. Reich?" she asked.

Nooo, Mom. Let that go! I won already!

"Dr. Reich? No, does he work here?" Dr. Fox asked.

"He's some kind of doctor my daughter found who cures cancer with electricity," she said. "Angela, tell him the list of all those vitamins you want me to take."

I opened my notebook and read from my blog-curated list, hoping my mom's latest interjection hadn't made Dr. Fox change his mind about her moving. He said yes to all my vitamins, even after he asked to see the exact "CoQ10" I was going to give my mom. I now know he asked that because I'd mispronounced it as C-Oh-Q-ten. That's carbon monoxide. He obviously didn't want to give me permission for that. But, still, he gave her his blessing to move across the country. He also patiently explained to me that physical therapists aren't only for athletes; they also teach patients ways to move to manage pain, like when you're sitting for hours on an airplane.

Before Dr. Fox exited, he left me, official mom-caretaking daughter, with one final order: "See if you can get your mom to take her pain meds," he said, with a grin on his face, like they'd had this fight before and he was passing me the honor of avenging his loss. I knew the battle of which he spoke. I never needed Nancy Reagan or fried eggs to warn me about drugs, my mom claimed she knew mothers who sold their bodies for marijuana. My mom prided herself on never needing anything stronger than Tylenol, even after cancer treatments. She was terrified just one taste of a prescription pain pill would pull her into addiction and make her lose her morals.

We left her doctor's office and instead of heading toward the parking lot, she motioned across a glass bridge to the hospital pharmacy.

"Let's get those pain pills now," Mom said.

Now that I was in charge, she seemed very eager to get high.

As we headed toward the pharmacy, my mom called her coworker to let her know she was coming in. I realized that my mom wasn't interested in just pain pills but also in her real drug of choice: her job.

I flanked her side like a bodyguard, ready for Overtime and Double Overtime to pop out from around every corner. In my eyes, everyone with a hospital badge was one of the Overtimes' accomplices. Those bitches would not win against me again.

I was right to be suspicious that my mom's willingness to take drugs was just a covert operation to keep working. As soon as we hit the hospital lobby, an older man in a valet uniform gave my mom a respectful head nod; in response, she yelled across the room, "My daughter wants me to take time off and go to Los Angeles!"

He simply said, "Well, that sounds nice," and my mom seemed taken aback that he didn't object more. The valet was probably wondering why I had subbed in for his favorite husband of faith who chauffeured my mom VIP style to the front door. Why I had her walking through hallways and over bridges like a peasant. He didn't know that my mom insisted we walk. He didn't know that I'd suspected Bill's chauffeured drop-offs weren't as much about love as they were about control.

The more I followed Mom's slow steps through the corridors, the more it became clear that she was one of those employees who had worked there so long she'd become part of the fabric of the hospital. She knew almost everyone with an ID badge. People noticed that she hadn't arrived on time. They expressed surprise she was walking through the halls, commenting that recently she seemed to stay in her office most of the day. Everyone wanted a moment of her time and she indulged everyone. She reminded me of the seasoned women at my jobs, the ones who could guide you through which assholes to avoid and calm you down in a bathroom stall before you cursed one of them out and got fired. Everyone my mom greeted seemed to need her there. She made their workday more tolerable.

I didn't give a damn what they needed, my job as newly minted caretaker was to get my mom out of there and on the plane to cancer healing as soon as possible. To me, the people greeting her were the same people who had seen her struggle and still let her work every day. She certainly had enough work friends that they could have united and formed a human chain around the hospital, refusing to let her work with stage 4 cancer.

While people enthusiastically greeted my mom, the first greeting aimed at me was . . . less enthusiastic, more: *Oh, shit. What's she doing back here?* A woman in scrubs hugged my mom and midhug, her eyes met mine and flickered with concern.

"And how you been doing, honey," she asked me, her tone implying that she really meant: *Are you a free woman or are you locked up with your crazy buddies over there?*

The *crazy buddies over there* were the hospital psych patients enjoying a ten-minute sunshine/smoke break; in college, I'd been one of them.

Psych patients on a break are easy to spot if you know what you're looking for. Most have on patient gowns but no remnants of physical medical treatments like wheelchairs or even a Band-Aid. Their feet are clad in thin foam slippers or lace-free sneakers because shoelaces and suicidal ideation don't mix, but also because it's hard to sprint away on a smoke break wearing shoes that aren't laced to your feet. Something being harder doesn't mean it's impossible, so occasionally my fellow psych patients ran for freedom during our breaks, giving everyone outside the hospital a live-action show. We patients who were too scared to run reacted with a mix of cheers, chasing, and/or crying, depending on how well our medication had been titrated. Then we'd all go back upstairs, eat with our sporks and recount how exciting our smoke break was to the new depressives who weren't yet allowed outside.

When I was one of those inpatients, my mom went from proudly pointing across the street at my dorm to sneaking visits to my locked psych ward after a shift. During the archaic days of the '90s, few people talked openly about mental health. Okay, a few A-list folks did and while they were usually lauded for being brave, those of us without magazine covers and millions of dollars kept that shit a secret. We used words like *nervous breakdown* and never admitted using antidepressants even though they were climbing the "most prescribed" chart every year.

Whenever my mom visited me, I could feel her shame. To her, my depression wasn't a misfiring of brain chemicals but a diagnosis that reflected poorly on her parenting. Once I was released, my inpatient treatment became one of those things she never brought up, perhaps for the same reason she kept her cancer a secret: It's simply easier to keep conversations to positive topics.

Though I had long since graduated to being a regular outpatient depressed person like most Americans, in the same hospital where I was once a patient, it was difficult for me to not imagine that Mom was remembering that version of me who had given up on life. *How could that girl take care of her?* As her friend in scrubs, Julie, continued asking how I was, I pointedly lowered my head, not in shame, but so she'd notice my shoes had shoelaces. If she needed more convincing, I'd challenge her to a Rorschach, then she could catch me in the cafeteria where no one tackled me when I grabbed a plastic knife. Julie didn't know I was hospitalized for depression, which meant, even at my worst, I could only hurt my mom if it's possible to sleep someone to death.

Just like Julie only knew one side of me, I could see she also didn't know the side of my mom that paused about every twenty steps to catch her breath. Now, every twenty steps someone else, like Julie, was stopping my mom so she could hide her breath-catching needs under her friends' needs to catch up. I had a feeling no one had formed a chain around the hospital because Mom had strategically hidden from them how ill she was just as she'd done with me. And here she was, hiding her illness again, insisting that someone talk her daughter out of her silly idea to "take a vacation to Los Angeles."

I followed my mom around as she made pit stops to her hospital friends, baiting each of them with reasons she couldn't leave work to go to Los Angeles with me. As she did, I gave them looks telegraphing that if they agreed with her, they'd have my crazy psych ward ass to deal with. Perhaps, because of that, no one objected to her "vacation."

Hours after she'd called her co-worker and told her she was coming in, we finally made our way to her office. Mom was concerned with everyone's opinions about her move, but mostly Ada's, who would be stuck with all her work.

5

Parable of the Parking Space

The office Mom shared with Ada was a shoebox; it had no windows and was smaller than the mental ward's isolation room. I stood in the doorway and tried to seem awestruck as my mom showed off her cramped quarters like it was a penthouse suite.

"Look at you and your own office!" I said. If she was proud, I was proud. But I was also prepared to call that tiny fire-trap what it was, if she tried to choose it over Los Angeles. She then shut the door on me, knowing I couldn't fit inside.

I put my ear to the door to eavesdrop on whether Ada was rebuking my mom about taking a "vacation" and leaving her with extra work. Unfortunately, their door was made from some thick Declaration of Independence–era Philadelphia wood, so I heard less than if I'd put a seashell to my ear. I gave up, but soon after, Ada exited and motioned me down the hallway.

"She's really moving to Los Angeles?" she asked, pulling me to a quiet corner.

"I hope so," I said, not sure if Ada was on my side.

"She better be. I've been telling her to take some time off," Ada continued, then whipped out her cell phone, instructing me to exchange numbers with her. "If your mom says one word about feeling guilty leaving me with work? Call me. I will sweetly straighten her ass out." Ada then smiled conspiratorially like we were secret allies against my mom's need to work.

"We got this," Ada said. "Most people don't know how stubborn she is," she added.

In that dark corner of the hospital, I hugged Ada, one of those *I just met you but you are now my sister* hugs. If anyone was forced to know my mom outside of her cheerful hallway persona that always insisted she was fine and had no complaints, it was Ada. Labored breathing, swollen lymph nodes, and a bad marriage can't be easily hidden in a tiny room where simply opening a door involved a game of Twister. With Ada's blessing, I hoped Mom would finally give in and go home to pack. Instead, her stubbornness geared up again.

"I'm not moving unless I can afford to pay you rent," she said. I gently argued that she didn't need to pay rent, but she dug in her heels and insisted we stop by the Benefits Office to see if there was any money Bill didn't take. As my mom told a woman named Barbara that her daughter was trying to "move her across the country with no job," I sat quietly and focused on posters touting the joys of teamwork until my mom quietly gasped.

"Oh my god, Angie," Mom said, looking at the computer screen the worker had swiveled toward her. "I have a disability policy." She laughed in disbelief at her luck. It was her quiet, self-conscious laugh, the one I knew meant she'd found a small, unexpected piece of joy. I hadn't heard that laugh since I'd arrived for the surprise visit that was supposed to be over by now. She wasn't laughing in apology or for bringing up a hard topic. She was genuinely beside herself that she could receive three years' salary just by filling out one form.

The disability money meant she could have some stability in the shaky state of California; with it, Mom could rest without worrying about accepting free help from me. I decided I'd charge her fifty dollars a month for rent and force her to use the rest to finally self-publish her book of poems. I'd then secretly buy all the copies with her rent payments so she'd think self-published poems can become bestsellers. This disability form was our golden ticket. I just needed to get the form signed by her doctor. I pounced on the printed-out form and hightailed it across that glass bridge like I wished I'd had the courage to run on my psych inpatient smoke breaks.

I returned to the Benefits Office, completely out of breath. I proudly held the signed paper above my head like a kid who had caught a foul ball only for Miss Barbara to quietly point out it wasn't complete and she couldn't process it. Only Barbara and I could see the incomplete part she was pointing to: Date of Expected Death. I decided Dr. Fox neglecting the most important blank on the disability form was another positive sign: He'd skipped that line because he didn't think my mom was going to die. Plus, if she was actually dying, why hadn't he mentioned that little fact during our visit?

I raced back across the bridge for the third time. The form was finally complete—with a death date six months in the future. Just like I'd convinced myself Dr. Fox had left it blank on purpose, I also convinced myself that Dr. Fox had picked a date out of thin air just to help us get the money. I mean, how could someone, even a doctor, know that death is exactly six months away? I damn near skipped back to the Benefits Office. I had, with that signed paper, given my mother everything she'd asked for. I rounded the corner like a bad-ass, ready to hand the form off to Barbara, but my mom was sitting outside of the Benefits Office. Their door was closed.

"I didn't want to keep Barbara past five," Mom said. "She said we can just mail it."

"No problem," I said and loaded her into the car. If she was going to make me work twice as hard, I'd do it like she did, with no complaints and a smile.

"Did we kick butt today or what?" I asked, as we navigated through rush hour traffic to the post office.

My mom simply nodded.

That wasn't enough for me. I wanted at least *Attagirl, you've come a long way from those foam slippers.* I tried again.

"Look at all those open spaces in front of the post office! We're magic together," I said, before noticing every single meter had a No Parking sign tied to it. I pulled up to one and parked anyway.

"It says no parking," she admonished me.

I lost my smile. "I see what it says," I said, with what my mom would call "bass" in my voice. I jumped out of the car.

"You can't park here," a young woman called out. She explained it was campus move out day. I replied that my mom trumped "rich fucking people moving." Upon hearing me curse, Mom hopped out of the car like her legs had sprouted pogo sticks. She looked around, apologizing with her eyes to the smattering of Ivy League families pushing moving carts.

"Angela, please just move the car."

"No, Mom, you please just get in the car," I said, wondering how shame over my cursing could make her legs work so well. I knew I was embarrassing her but I continued to meet her stubbornness with more of my own, both of us determined not to back down first.

"Mom, sometimes, I get to decide what's best. You are more important than people moving minifridges!"

The volunteer looked as if the university hadn't prepared her that there may be mother-daughter fights on her shift and as she summoned an older man in an official Parking Authority uniform for backup, I embarrassed my mom even more by sprinting away from all of them and into the post office as she apologized for me. If I couldn't get my *attagirl*, I'd at least use her apologetic nature as a defense weapon while I secured her three years of pay. And finally, we had everything we officially needed, but when I drove off from the post office, instead of applause, my mom chastised me.

"You didn't have to get so angry back there."

"And I wish you'd get angrier," I snapped back. "I am angry," I replied, listing everything I had to be angry about: her hiding her pain from everyone, her hiding how bad her marriage was, her constant praising of Bill when I was trying to give and not take like he did and Jesus H. Christ, could she not give me some props?

"Why shouldn't I be angry?" I asked, going on to use "I feel" statements just like I'd learned in both marriage counseling and the psych ward.

"I feel you don't believe I can help you get better. I feel like you love Bill more than you love me. I feel you always praise him, but with me, it's just shame and stubbornness. Why can't you trust me like you trusted him?" I needed her to say she trusted me so that I would trust myself. It was the type of awkward emotional moment that would happen often as I learned to become her caretaker. I wanted her to know that I was grown and capable, but I also was still the little girl who needed her approval.

"Bill's going to take my house if I move!" she said, in a voice louder than I'd heard all weekend. "I messed up with him, I really messed up. I worked so hard for that house," she said, embarrassed.

And just like the needy kid I was pretending not to be, I thought, *Yes! It's someone else she doesn't trust, not me!* while I rubbed her back, grateful she had finally admitted her concern.

"I won't let Bill take your house. If he can't even manage to get the right fake degree, how is he going to take your house?" I said, promising to fight him with all the anger she told me she hated. I told her all she needed to do was talk to me, tell me honestly everything she needed, and I'd figure out a way to do every damn thing. I pulled over and put the car in park. I was not moving until I got her to open up. I knew with my mom, the emotionally honest part of the cancer fight might be as tough as the cancer itself.

She tiptoed through a simple list of wants: a few days to pack, that we bring her dogs with us and find a new home for the birds. Having greased the wheels with the animals' needs, besides saving her house, she had only one other need for herself. She requested our flight be first class. I'd flown her that way to Antigua and had told her to get used to premium service being the norm. I'd meant it back then when I had money.

"The physical therapist said first-class seats are better for my circulation," my mom explained.

I nodded—*say no more*—and then booked two first-class *adjacent* seats: the second row of economy plus. Her physical therapist might have said first class, but my credit card balance said no.

"We're all booked," I announced. "Five days from now we'll be two single ladies in Hollywood," I said, even though I wasn't technically single. Alas, just like my mom didn't need to know my credit card was maxed out, there was also no need for her to know I was shacked up with Byron, my boyfriend of eight months: Cohabitating with a man before marriage was something best kept under wraps from church women of a certain age. While I respected her Christian morality meter, Jesus, unlike me, had no student loan debt, had a carpenter father who could build him a house, and he had twelve homies to split rent with while living in the low-cost city of Bethlehem. In expensive-ass Los Angeles, after one good date with a man who had pay stubs and seemed at least 72 percent sane, I'd be like *So, sexy high roller, wanna shack up?* Mom was lucky she hadn't needed to move in a year ago, when a one-night stand had turned into a monthlong squatter I was only able to extricate by force. After evicting him, he still lived in my driveway for a bit and would text me about how badly his life was going.

Him: C'mon. Let me in. I lost my job for showing up late.

I thought, *How the hell can you live in your car and be late for work?*

Basically, I'd begged my mom to be completely honest with me but that didn't mean I was going to do the same. I nervously called Byron, explaining that my short surprise trip had evolved into Mom and her two dogs moving in. Byron was eager to help, even saying he could arrange to have a friend install handicap bars in the guest bathroom and asked if there was anything else he could do.

"Yes, you can hide all your man shit downstairs," I said. I knew if my mom saw evidence of any cohabitation, despite all we'd gone through to get her to Los Angeles, she'd use those handicap bars to hoist herself right on up and out of my house of sin.

6

Raising Canes and Telling Lies

As Byron kept me updated on how many body sprays he'd hidden away in the garage, I got more practice in lying. I was quite good at it, perhaps having a head start from being the daughter of a mother who kept problems close to her chest. When I started thinking back to my childhood, I realized that even before cancer, anything even remotely negative, she'd find a way to cover up. Soon after she'd split from my father, instead of telling us that money was tight, she told Jack and me that if we wanted our allowances, we could get them by collecting cans.

"I bet you two find so many cans, you'll make double your allowances!" she said, hyping us up before putting us in the back seat to go on a soda can hunt.

"If we get pulled over, wave and smile at the cops," Mom instructed us. She was driving on expired tags and frequently explained that a mom won't get arrested if her kids wave at the cops. Sure enough, as we were collecting cans, she did get pulled over and my brother and I waved and smiled at that cop like he was passing by us on a parade float. The cop quickly let our mom go with only a warning. It wasn't until I was an adult that I figured out that Mom had lied and not every mother could evade arrest via kids who waved; it worked for ours because two half-white kids in the back seat waving at a cop passively let him know that if he caused problems with the Black woman driving, there would be a white man somewhere he'd have to deal with.

After our high yellowness set us free and we'd reached the recycling plant, my brother and I anticipated all the dollar bills we'd get as Mom handed over seven can-filled trash bags. We didn't get one single dollar bill. Just some coins and a kind lecture that the plant only recycles aluminum cans. We thought all cans were aluminum.

"And what did we learn about soda cans today?" Mom quizzed us as if collecting cans was never about her money anxiety, but an interactive lesson on how most 1980s soda cans were actually not aluminum but made from steel and tin. She also gave us our allowances anyway.

There were other lies, like when she took us to the animal shelter and said it was "just a different kind of zoo than the (too expensive) zoo we were used to." Thinking back to the den of well-intentioned lies she raised me in made me feel more at ease with the half-truths I often found myself telling her.

"No, I don't mind driving you all around Philly to say bye to every person you've ever met in a thrift store."

I hadn't actually minded; I'd minded the chaos it caused. Philadelphia's narrow one-way streets were originally designed for horses, slave trade auctions, and cracking Liberty Bells. They were not designed for 2.3 million people in cars. Certainly not 2.3 million short-tempered Philadelphians in cars being held up by us as my mom slowly hoisted herself out of her car. The people trapped behind us on those one-way streets would express their disapproval in honks, which often escalated to cursing as I further held them up to wait until my mom was safely inside before I drove off.

"Fucking move!" a woman behind me had shrieked.

"No, you fucking wait!" I'd yelled back, then, of course, had to apologize to Mom for cursing. Even if I didn't curse and simply did what I thought a good daughter should do—help her out of the car—I'd have to apologize for making her look disabled, which would take up even more time as she shooed me back into the car while saying, "As long as God gave me two working legs, I'm going to use them."

After only one day of street bickering with both my mom and strangers, I knew I had to make sure the next day wasn't the same. As Mom went over the next day's itinerary, I lied and told her the people she wanted to visit preferred to visit her.

"Yep, Aunt Nina wants to come here. She hasn't been to the city in a while," I lied. I hadn't even talked to Aunt Nina and as far as I knew, my aunt Nina moved to rural Jersey to get far away from the exact curse outs I'd just been through. She was much happier on her thirty acres where she fed birds and cleaned her shotguns. She was a proud woman with a soft, yet to-the-point manner of speaking that made my mom's stubbornness go into hiding. Aunt Nina had also recently started using a cane. As soon as I lied to my mom about Aunt Nina wanting to visit Philadelphia, I snitched to Aunt Nina telling her how my mom thought canes made her look disabled. How I was trying to be the perfect daughter and caretaker, but doing so would be easier if she could get my mom to use a cane.

Aunt Nina arrived with her cane; it was wood and hand-carved, none of that basic aluminum gray for a fly lady like her. For about an hour, we chitchatted with my mom about all the fun she'd have visiting me in California and Mom even scribbled down Aunt Nina's recommendations for fun things to do. As Aunt Nina readied to leave, my mom again waved away my help getting up from her seat. I glanced at Aunt Nina.

"Use this," my aunt said, handing her cane to my mom. "My son's enough cane for me," she went on, nodding at my cousin John. Cousin John was football player size; twice when visiting me in Los Angeles tourists had asked for his autograph, reasoning a man built like a superhero must at least be famous in some way. Even if my cousin failed at being a human cane, his six-foot-two, two-hundred-pound frame could certainly act as my aunt's crash pad. My cousin was probably thinking, *Thanks, fam, now I gotta navigate my wobbly mom down these dark-ass Philly row house steps without a cane,* but I was grateful my wobbly mom was finally steady and I'd figure out a way to make it up to John later. As soon as they drove off, my mom dropped the cane by the front door and shuffled back to her seat.

"Too bad it won't fit in my suitcase," she said.

"It's a cane. You don't pack it. It's like an arm, it stays with you."

She ignored me and left her new arm abandoned in the entryway before pulling herself slowly up the stairs to pack. Even though she gripped the banister like she was climbing Mt. Everest, she flashed me a triumphant smile showing me she didn't need my help and she certainly didn't need no cane.

Still, I knew Mom wouldn't leave the cane in Philly. It would be bad etiquette to reject a gift plus I'd have no qualms snitching to my aunt about that too.

At the airport, it only took a short time for a kind wheelchair attendant, Melody, to cajole Mom into being pushed to the gate. My mom held the cane in her lap as she and Melody were directed into a special screening area. In the minutes I waited for them, I imagined Mom was second-guessing our trip and citing some study that contraindicates recent cancer treatment with whatever the hell is in our airport security scanners. I was so relieved when she exited that I didn't notice she had again ditched the cane until twenty minutes before our flight was boarding.

My mom claimed leaving the cane at security was a mistake but still nonchalantly hoped that "it would go to someone who really needs it." I hurried back to security, determined to retrieve her cane.

A supervisor stopped me midsentence. "If it's your mom's cane, *she* has to come back and get it," he said coldly and turned back to his paperwork about a bowling ball he'd accidentally logged as a bomb or whatever he thought was more important than my mom's cane.

"Sir, she literally can't walk back to get it. It's a walking cane. For *walking* back to get things."

"You said that," he said, his eyes not leaving the paperwork on his desk. "I can't give you someone else's belongings. What if you saw someone leave a laptop then claimed it was yours?"

Are we really playing a "what if" game when I have twenty minutes to board? "People would try to claim a laptop because it's valuable," I argued, but he had no appreciation for my debate about how there was no gang of thieves in all of history who focused exclusively on canes. He was set on following the rules even though the rules didn't work for people the rule makers didn't even think of, like a woman who couldn't physically walk back to claim a lost item.

"She really needs it," I begged, my voice starting to rise. Travelers threw me side-eyes as they put on their shoes and quickly navigated their luggage away from the woman causing a ruckus at security.

"She can get it on her return flight," the supervisor said, assuming that we were two normal people who were going on a trip with a set return date. One where we'd be back in Philadelphia soon with unwanted "Hollywood" T-shirts for our friends.

"We don't have a return flight. She has stage 4 cancer!" I yelled as tears started rolling down my cheeks. Admitting my mom may never return to Philadelphia felt like admitting that the hope I had for her cancer to go into remission or be cured was another lie on top of all the little ones that carried us to the airport. I stood there, tears streaming down my cheeks, hoping one of the faces in the crowd would at least ask if I was okay. They continued averting their eyes. Until Melody, the wheelchair attendant, busted through the security crowd.

"Give her her mom's cane," she called out. Loudly. The same short-tempered Philly loud that had exasperated me driving my mom around was suddenly my ally. Melody put her arm around me and continued, telling the officer he was "taking his job too damn serious," which made him stand up from his desk and shove the cane at me.

"You just cost me my job," he reprimanded both of us, then he stomped back to his desk.

Melody offered me a crumpled-up tissue.

"Fuck him and his job. You better hurry, your flight's about to board," Melody said, waving away my expressions of gratefulness. I'd imagined that in a cancer fight, a village of people like Melody would gather behind us, forming a big pink supportive walkathon. I imagined they'd cheer us on and have our backs as we faced all the small daily struggles the medical research talked nothing about. I had no idea that there would be so many moments when those struggles were just a sideshow for strangers to judge. As Melody hurried back to her post, I felt immensely grateful. I promised myself I'd no longer be a person who averts their eyes or judges others' problems. The world needs more loud-ass Melodies.

Cane in hand, I dipped quickly into the nearest bathroom, making sure that I'd have no trace of tears when I returned to my mom's side. Tears erased, I sat next to her and put the cane between our chairs. *There. I did it.*

"I bet you gave them hell," she said.

"Nah, it was fine. Easy," I lied, as we gathered up our carry-ons and the cane to board our (almost) first-class flight.

———

Once in LA, as we rode to my house, I was forced to lie again. I'd answered an unknown number because I always answered unknown numbers; as a very unemployed person, every call could have been the headhunter that saved me from being back collecting cans. I was close enough to going back that I already web-searched recycling rates in California and learned I was only eighty thousand cans away from being current on my bills.

"Hello," I said, happy to give my mom a taste of my highly

practiced, confident professional voice. The unknown caller was not a job offer, but my mortgage company, more specifically, their poor people section. Months earlier, I'd learned that my taxes went toward bailing banks out and in return, the banks were expected to refinance some of their crappy adjustable-rate mortgages. Mine fit that definition so I'd filled out more than thirty-five pages of paperwork in an attempt to lower my monthly mortgage payments. Those thirty-five pages turned into one hundred five pages as my paperwork was lost three times. I would commiserate online with other struggling homeowners in a forum where the most replied-to posts had titles like, "F%^&! They Lost My Paperwork Again," or "Bank of America Is the Devil." Interspersed between every hundred or so complaints, someone would post a success story and we'd run them off the site asking for too many details in hopes one of them would give out a secret code on how they'd gotten their banks to do what the government ordered and saved their house.

Part of the application process was to give my mortgage company access to my bank and credit card statements. After seven months of making sure the most frivolous item on my statement was a store-bought birthday cake, I worried that this sudden call was a *Gotcha! You charged an economy plus ticket instead of a regular one! You're not broke!* Then the loan officer would hang up and my mom and I would immediately be forced to live under an ADA-compliant bridge. If I asked the loan officer to call me back, I knew I would never hear from her again, but I also knew letting my mom know I didn't even have the basics of life she'd always taught me to have, like the ability to pay my bills, was not a conversation I was ever planning to have.

She was the first person I bragged to after I bought my house, even reading to her from my deed, which stated "Owner: Angela Nissel, an unmarried woman." I wanted her to know I'd taken her advice and purchased the house in my own name so I couldn't ever lose it to the man I was about to marry. When she'd visited me shortly after my divorce, Mom told me how proud she was. "At least you have two things a man can never take from you: a house and a degree."

If my husband had wanted my anthropology degree in the divorce, I'd rather have given that to him than all the money he was allowed by law. Unlike my mom's nursing degree, there was not a huge demand for degrees whose recipients' only skills are giving level-101 lectures about the Himalayan culture of tea.

To keep my mom in the dark about the poverty nature of the phone call, I responded to the loan officer's questions with vague, clipped answers, sounding much like a kidnapping victim secretly calling 911 when her abductor is within earshot.

"Are you unemployed, a seasonal worker, or disabled?" the loan officer asked.

"The first one," I replied hoping she wouldn't ask in detail about how unemployed I was. If she did, my mom would know I hadn't even made it to the second round of interviews to sell dinosaur-shaped earrings at a local museum.

"How much do you have in savings?"

"Nope," I simply replied.

Satisfied that my clipped answers had outwitted my mom, I hung up. My mom immediately asked, "Are you behind on your mortgage?"

"Of course not," I said, still cheery. We were in Los Angeles on the highway, what was she going to do, run? Her cane was in the trunk.

I changed the topic to all the thrift stores we were going to hit, only to have Mom interrupt me as we pulled onto my block.

"Is that a man taking photos of your house?"

"Probably paparazzi waiting for someone," I said. *Just another day in sunny Hollywood!*

No one famous lived in my neighborhood. The highlight of my neighborhood's Wikipedia entry is a man who served one term in Congress fifty years ago. I hoped my mom didn't know that once you start missing payments, the bank hires people to take photos of your home's condition, probably to make sure you don't burn it down before they kick you out.

The first sound my mom heard once we entered my underwater, pre-foreclosed home was Byron shouting "No! No!!" as he separated my eighty-pound mutt, Woody, from my mom's feisty Chihuahuas. My dog was not happy at having two roommates. The shelter had promised Woody was good with other dogs, but he wasn't. He hated dogs like they were the ones that put him in the shelter. Having Mom's dogs around would be a constant game of trying to get him not to break through the baby gate to eat her dogs for snacks.

"Mom, I told you about Byron. He's only here taking care of the dogs until we got here," I lied.

"I hope my babies didn't cause you too much trouble, Byron," she said and thanked him before retreating to her bedroom where she sat on the edge of the bed. I placed her dogs next to her where they each fought for space to squish their heads into her lap.

"Who are these for?" Mom asked later, noticing the newly installed grab bars along the toilet and shower. "You didn't have to do all this for me, but thank you," she said, finally giving me the kudos I'd selfishly wanted during all the battles of the past week.

"No, thank you," I said. And said it again as she questioned why on earth I was thanking her. I was thanking her for making the trip, for trusting that I could help her beat this triple-negative cancer. Being so focused on saving her life made my other problems pale in comparison. At that moment, I couldn't give a damn about the mortgage or the career—things that previously were at the top of my worry list. It was one of those moments where I believed in the stupid saying "everything happens for a reason." If my life was still going "perfectly" and I was hustling to please a boss and pay bills, I wouldn't be able to quietly sit and watch as my mom fell asleep. As she snored like a truck, I curled up right beside her, certain that we'd gotten through the hardest parts and that both of our lives were about to change for the better.

7

Wayward Daughter and Celebrity Doctors

In the first days of our new California life, my mom and I practiced being ladies of leisure: We slept in, we had pizza delivered, and our most emotionally taxing activity was trying to guess verdicts on judge shows. Mom bought a new wig and then decided it made her look like a "disabled hooker" so we practiced styling the tiny Afro that chemo had gifted her with. We bought rolling shopping baskets and she used her cane to navigate flea markets where she dropped vintage clothes like they were hot and full of bees.

"They must be crazy charging fifty dollars for a skirt I threw away decades ago," Mom whispered before reminiscing about her skirt that had seen both a Martin Luther King speech and a college first date. She had gotten so used to her cane that she had no problems leaning on it with one hand and tossing the skirt back through the other.

I told her the flea market visit was not for purchasing items but for retail reconnaissance; we'd learn our competitors' prices then undercut them once we opened Our Little Boutique. We also daydreamed aloud about how once we found the right doctor and my mom got better, we'd use some of our profit to start a Christian-based PI service that brought down men who preyed on nice church ladies.

In those first few days my mom lived with me, she and Byron became fast friends. If she suspected Byron lived with me, she said nothing. She did make him sit by her side as she planned our wedding, not knowing he and I had barely figured out who pays what portion of which utility bill, and unlike her, I was content to never give marriage a second chance. Mom also said nothing about me being unemployed, probably because some mornings I'd get dressed and go to what I told her was work. She didn't need to know the work was volunteer and involved shoveling horse shit at a rescue barn. When I returned home, I'd immediately shower so my mom couldn't sniff out that I didn't smell like success.

One night, as my mom got ready for bed, I noticed she had two space heaters running full blast. I turned them off as they were racking up kilowatt hours I could not afford. Minutes later, I heard her yell my name and I bolted back into her room to see her shivering like my walls were lined in ice, despite wearing thick pajamas.

"What happened? It's so cold," she said, her teeth chattering.

"Oops, I must have unplugged the heater. Sorry."

From that moment on, I let her keep both heaters running twenty-four seven and did not give one more single fuck about the bill.

After those few days of leisure came our first cancer must-do, an appointment with Dr. Singh, a well-respected Los Angeles oncologist. My mom and I drove to the area of Los Angeles where people with imported brick driveways resided. The helicopters overhead were no longer "ghetto birds" but traffic-phobic billionaires cruising to their lunch dates.

"Your new doctor must be amazing if she can afford rent around here," I said, as Mom marveled at how every other car was a Porsche or better. Upon meeting Dr. Singh, she certainly looked the part of a luxury oncologist. Her face seemed poreless, her pantsuit was tailored, and despite wearing stilettos, she glided into our patient room as if she were on roller skates. Certainly, Hollywood was gearing up to give her either a talk show or her own brand of vitamins. If anyone could force my mother's cancer into remission it was Dr. Singh. Perhaps, I speculated at the time, if I didn't get steady work in a few more months, I'd take a chance at medical school. Dr. Singh made the debt seem worth it. Just her presence gave me hope, as well as the fact that she'd read through my mom's BCB and still gave us an appointment. Dying people don't need doctor's appointments.

"How are you feeling today, Mrs. Nissel?" Dr. Singh asked while sitting on the stool across from us.

"So-so," my mom replied. I rarely heard her reply to a health professional with anything other than "blessed" or "great." "So-so" was the equivalent of "I'm in searing pain but I'm trying to hide it so I don't burden my daughter."

Dr. Singh reached for her stethoscope. "Do you mind if I remove your scarf?" she asked, and after my mom's reluctant nod, the doctor gingerly unwrapped the scarf from her neck exposing the angry lumps I'd only recently seen myself.

Dr. Singh eyes softened as she took in the lumps my mom had always gone to great lengths to hide. The look on the doctor's face showed that despite being one of the best in her field, what she saw still rattled her. She retied my mom's scarf in silence and put her stethoscope to the side. "You poor thing," she said, holding my mom's gaze.

"Yeah," my mom said as she dropped her eyes down to the fringe of her scarf.

"She's cold a lot too," I said as if that wasn't something the doctor could glean on her own from both the BCB and the layers of clothes Mom was wearing. I thought I was helping, making sure Dr. Singh had all the facts she needed to plot out my mom's curative plan. I was also just blabbing because I was uncomfortable at how morose the room had become.

"I'm going to give you a hospice referral, is that okay?" the doctor asked tenderly. My mother nodded in agreement. I immediately objected.

"We didn't move you across the country to put you in a home," I said, once again being a medical dunce. I thought a hospice was a physical place where terminal people go to die. Once the doctor and my mom corrected me and explained that hospice could be at home, I still denied my mom's need for it. If she really needed hospice, why hadn't anyone mentioned it before we'd traveled twenty-five hundred miles away from her home?

"I want the hospice," Mom said, and before I could object again, she quietly reminded me that I'd promised I'd give her anything she wanted. I'd meant fun shit like paying someone to shove Bill down a flight of steps or opening our thrift store. Not hospice. Not death. Rationally, I knew that one day she would die because we all die, but hiring a hospice service meant we accepted it was coming soon and were even laying out a welcome mat. It meant we'd completely given up hope. Her "Save the Tatas" T-shirts didn't say shit on the care tags about including death, so even though I agreed with hospice out of respect, I felt my mom wanting it was simply her being tired of fighting. I was not tired. The hospice referral just made me more determined to find another way to save her. I couldn't even think of her not being there. Besides finally having her all to myself, she was also giving my life purpose, a reason that I could accept as to why I had little else to look after.

Back in the car, the hum of traffic lulled my mom to sleep while her phone continually rang with names I recognized from her hospital goodbye tour. As she slept through the ringing, some of them started calling me. I ignored them. There was no way to say, *Yeah, everything's great, except the fancy LA doctor I promised? She just told my mom her treatment plan is to stay Black and die.*

Once back home, I told Mom I would do as she wanted and call the referral, but that I'd also be calling City of Hope. City of Hope had commercials full of bald patients smiling at their doctors, grateful for their expertise in rare and aggressive forms of cancer. No one got sent to hospice in their commercials.

"Really? You think they can help?"

"Yeah, they cure a lot of people," I said. I didn't even know if the patients on the commercials were actors. All I knew was they were people who weren't dead. I emailed City of Hope as we sat together with her dogs, soaking in the California sun.

"I know if there's any chance for treatment, you'll find a way to grab it," my mom said, her eyes following the sun setting behind the palm trees as she fell asleep again. Her energy levels seemed to drop a bit each day. In a week she'd gone from slowly navigating flea markets to becoming winded simply by standing up for too long. Even though her body was slower, her mind remained sharp. Between naps, she wrote poems and read her Bible. In her sixty-four years of life, other than our Antigua trip, I had never seen her so at ease.

After I scheduled a hospice home visit, my mom teased me. "I know you'll have a notebook full of questions to ask the referral lady," she said.

"I just want to make sure the service gives you good care," I said.

The referral lady. A service.

I imagined we were both choosing our words carefully to avoid saying "hospice." The absence of the word was almost as glaring as simply saying it; we'd never used shorthand for other workers that came into a house. A plumber was never "that guy with the pipes," but we used synonyms with hospice because speaking aloud about death being a possibility felt taboo.

Rose, the hospice nurse, arrived. She had the demeanor of someone who wished she was a hospice client and not a nurse. The best way to describe her personality is she'd seen so many people die she went home and prayed for it to happen to her so she wouldn't have to go over the insurance benefits chart one more damn time. Rose kept talking about insurance like she was very concerned, despite us having a referral from a high-end doctor, that we couldn't afford to pay.

Maybe she'd gotten written up for signing up too many hospice hoboes? Maybe it's extremely difficult to collect money from people who are soon to be dead? But then she shushed my mom. Literally shushed her for asking a question. Despite me wanting to shove her ass right out the door on the spot, I was afraid to upset Mom, to be too angry. I also, medically ignorant as usual, wasn't sure if we had a choice in hospice care. I thought a referral was set in stone, so we signed up with Rose despite her shush.

"What did you think of her?" my mom asked, reading over one of the brochures Rose had left behind.

"Hated her."

"I wouldn't say I hated her—" Mom said.

"Because you'd never say *hate*," I said and told her I was going online to find another hospice.

The same internet whose reviews helped me decide on vitamins, banks, and fancy LA doctors morphed into being as helpful as the Yellow Pages when it came to hospice. There were lots of ads but very few personal reviews. Perhaps people aren't in a reviewing mood after using hospice services. *Mom had a good death! Five stars! Would use again!* Despite hospices having few online reviews, I found solace in the general internet consensus that hospice workers were the unsung heroes of the medical world. Rose and her shushing were an anomaly. I decided to pick the first hospice that, unlike Rose's, had correct spelling on their website.

Donna showed up and was the exact five-star hospice angel I'd read about. She was about my mom's age and her frizzy blond hair and stained scrubs let me know that, like my mom, she probably put her patients first and herself last. *Perfect!* Talking with Donna was like chatting with a friend who was overly interested in my mom's comfort and bowel movements. It was cozy. She was cheery. After a few days it was more like an aunt was coming over and not a doula of impending death. Still, while Mom and Donna made daily small talk, I'd sit on the toilet, refreshing my email and hoping that City of Hope would reply so I could fire sweet Donna. While waiting for City of Hope's reply, I'd surf around making sure there weren't any other possible cancer treatments. I'd never forgive myself if I left one curative stone unturned.

I skipped over ads promising secret cancer cures doctors didn't want me to know about. I believe there is too much prestige and money to be made in curing cancer for any doctor to hide a cure. I did start to believe that doctors were hiding that fasting could cure cancer because there was no money and prestige in a cure that is essentially free. As I read that fasting reduces glucose levels and reduced glucose levels make it harder for cancer to grow, even though I barely knew what glucose was, I knew that I had to convince my mom to go to the California desert and fast until her hunger pains ate that cancer away. *We didn't give up on modern medicine, modern medicine gave up on us!* we'd say with a raised fist, once she was sufficiently starving and cured. I found a place where for thousands of dollars a week, they would feed us only juice and we'd do daily affirmations about my mom's health. I wasn't sure how I would pitch this desert trip to a mom who could barely stay awake more than a few hours a day.

———

Unable to reach my mother, her friends and co-workers kept calling me. I always told them she was resting, not going into details about how she pretty much rested all day. Their understanding responses gave me reasons to regather some hope. They were happy she was resting. They told me not to worry, that we all sleep more when we get older. They guessed that her pain medication was knocking her out and when her body got used to it, she'd be back on her feet. I never told them that she was now so weak, I helped her the few steps from her bed to the plastic commode and I also bathed her. She didn't want me to bathe her, but I always, proudly, won the fight.

"Stop fighting me, I like helping you," I said. I'm sure Mom thought that was another one of my lies, but it was not. Her letting me bathe and wipe her ass felt like an honor, like the most important thing in the world. When she got stubborn about accepting any of my help because I didn't need to see "her big behind," I'd pull my pants to my ankles and start straightening her room until my bare behind made her more uncomfortable than letting me see hers. Then, while she slept, I'd sit by her side, hug her dogs, and feel nothing but gratefulness that they were all there. In those quiet moments, where I was concentrating on small comforts like keeping the dogs quiet so she could rest, I couldn't ignore the nagging feeling that the fasting cure would be just another failure added on to my list of potential cures. Still, I couldn't decide whether a good daughter stays in the present and is grateful for the small moments we had left or if real love keeps striving for the next supposed cure.

———

Within days of my mom starting hospice, the City of Hope called me back.

"I'm sorry, there's nothing the doctor can do," the receptionist said. My mom's cancer was too far gone. I didn't ask what the difference was between her stage 4 and that lady they showed off on their City of Hope website. I knew just like most things cancer, I wouldn't understand. I did understand that the word *hope* was bullshit, something dangled in front of struggling people when there was nothing left that could help.

"You were my last chance," I said to the City of Hope reception-ist while breaking down into tears. "I really wish you guys would change your name."

As my mom slept that night, I gave up on hope. Instead of searching for more cures, I sat on the toilet and tried the only thing I hadn't yet: I prayed for a miracle from her God.

"I know you haven't heard from me in a while, but I promise you if you take my mom from me, I won't be able to handle it." I told God that if he took her away, I was certain that I would die too.

8

Resurrection and Cheesecake

The next day, God showed he takes suicidal toilet prayers seriously. When I awoke, my mom was more alert than she'd been in days; she was on her feet and performing her love language of choice, cleaning every surface she could reach.

When I was younger, she'd flood our childhood house with music and turn washing windows and floors into an old school R&B party of one. As I got older, she'd clean my apartments, the not-so-hidden message in her dusting and polishing being, *I'm proud of you but, Lord, if someone sees these countertops they'll think I raised you in a mud hut.* I used to ask her not to clean, saying I'd get to it on one of my few days off. It was a way of reminding her that instead of being embarrassed by my dirt, she should be proud that I, like her, was working too hard to even notice it until someone else brought it up. For her to be cleaning meant both she and our mother-daughter dynamic had returned to normal. Normal was miraculous.

I stared at my mom for a moment as she hand-washed dishes despite there being a dishwasher two steps to her left. She looked at me like her being awake and standing upright without help was nothing out of the ordinary.

"What? I'm not just going to live in your house without helping," she said, gesturing to the clean kitchen as evidence of help I'd never asked for.

"You okay?" I asked, not sure what else to ask when witnessing a miracle.

"Yeah, your dishes were dirty."

"But—how'd you get out of bed?"

She looked at me quizzically. "With my feet."

And then we stood there in that awkward moment where two people in a conversation realize it's going absolutely nowhere and the only option is for one of you to disengage. I decided not to waste time with questions and to enjoy that God had answered my prayers and I had my mom back. She finished the dishes and went into her room to call her friends. I picked up her slack, dialing up people whose calls I had ignored, gushing about her improvement. Any nervousness they had over her unreturned calls turned into collective exhales.

"If you could see how well she cleaned my pans," I said, explaining how I'd talked to God from the commode the night before.

"Won't he do it."

"We've been praying too."

"Thank you, Jesus."

By noon, Mom hadn't even nodded off for a second. It was like time had reversed; she and her pups went back and forth between the living room TV and the patio, and instead of fighting me over seeing her butt, she was back to our normal fighting about not wanting to be in charge of what we ate for lunch.

"Don't matter to me. Whatever you want is fine," she said.

"We'll both starve then," I said, knowing she didn't want me to starve and secretly also knowing that each second she didn't eat meant one more second for her glucose levels to destroy the cancer that already seemed to be retreating.

"Okay, well, maybe—can we have cheesecake?" my mom asked, her mouth turning up into a half smile for daring to request a dessert item for lunch.

In the past few days, she'd only eaten sparingly; I'd started supplementing her meals with nutrition shakes. Food delivery apps were still a few years off, so I left my mom's side to drive and gather up celebratory cheesecake. It was the first time I'd left the house in over a week. As I stepped into the bright California sun, I felt as though God was shining down his light particularly on us. Even the varied supermarket selection of cheesecakes seemed like a sign that life is inherently bountiful. I charged three slices of cheesecake, each with a different topping, practicing how I'd demand Mom not ask me which one I wanted and take her first choice. I was so grateful about getting another chance to spoil her, I even decided I'd find a church to take her to on Sunday. Hell, I'd even join the church. If talking to God once from a toilet could do this much, I'd have to give in and say my mom was right about Jesus being both the way and the light.

Cheesecake procured, I drove back toward my home and saw lights. This wasn't that Jesus light, but flashing red ones. They belonged to an ambulance stopped outside my front door.

No, no, no, no, no.

My heart pounded as I thought of the thousand things that could have gone wrong in the ten minutes I was gone. The ambulance and accompanying fire truck were blocking the road, so I parked in the middle of the street. I flung open my car door hard enough to snap it off, feet flying toward my front door so I could get a view of what my overgrown tree was blocking. Through the canopy of leaves, I could see glimpses of uniformed firefighters kneeling in a half circle around my front door. When I reached my front lawn, I saw that my mom was in the middle of their half circle, lying flat on her back at the bottom of my two front steps.

A fireman approached me. He held his hand out to stop me from coming closer, perhaps assuming that I was a lookie-loo.

"Do you know this woman?"

"That's my mom!" I said, noticing her pants were around her ankles, exposing her diaper. She was, thankfully, alert and alive, but looked far from the miracle mom I had left. Her terrified eyes darted around until she locked eyes with me.

"Where did you go?" she asked.

I have failed at many moments in my life, but the tremble in her voice when she asked me that one question made me feel like I was God's biggest failure and that he was getting me back for daring to pray to him. I hated myself as I looked down on her, embarrassed to even meet her eyes.

"She asked me to get cheesecake," I explained to the EMTs. I started apologizing because I was certain that they, with all their medical training, were smarter than me and knew that you never leave a hospice patient alone to get cheesecake, even if she had, overnight, transformed back into the self-reliant mom you've always known.

"She tripped over her pants," a fireman said. "We have to take her to the hospital, but she won't go."

I kneeled down to my mom's side, proud that she was at least strong enough to tell a group of men in uniform what she didn't want to do.

"Don't let them take me," she whispered.

"You can't take her," I said to the firemen.

"We have to take her."

"But it's going to hurt," Mom cried, completely back to the mom whose body felt searing pain at any movement. Once again, I found myself desperately wanting to give her anything she asked for, but this time I couldn't. Standing with a bag full of cheesecake felt stupid as shit when I was forcing her to lose more of her autonomy.

"I'm so, so sorry, Mom," I repeated over and over, furrowing my brow to squeeze back the tears, reasoning that you can't fuck up like I just did and cry, especially when she wasn't. Mom's eyes were dry. She was only gritting her teeth and preparing for the pain of her sore body being rolled onto a gurney.

"You've been through worse pain, Mom. It'll be five seconds," I said, knowing it was just another one of my lies. I didn't know her pain; who the hell was I to tell her what she could tolerate? The EMTs gently wrapped a blanket around her as a thin shock absorber from their touch. As they carefully unrolled her from the blanket onto the gurney, she winced as if she were being rolled onto a bed of nails. She whimpered over every bump as we drove to the ER. I held her hand and tried to use humor to distract her from the pain I'd caused.

"Why were you outside? You finally could walk and your first move was to run away from me?" I laughed.

"Someone rang your doorbell," she said, an answer just as plain as why she had been washing my dishes: Something needed to be done, so she'd done it.

"I'm so so sorry," I said, angry at whoever had rung the doorbell, but even angrier at myself for not thinking of disconnecting the doorbell when I left the house. Why had I been so busy trying to understand science when I didn't even know simple shit like that?

———

While Mom was being seen by a doctor, I paced the emergency room lobby. Jen, a hospice supervisor, arrived, having been alerted that a patient under her care was being transported to the hospital. I felt like a wayward kid being called by the principal when Jen approached me. Her eyes were heavy with fatigue. It was clear that the day had already taken its toll on her. I hated being another burden, so I fumbled around, trying, once again, to apologize and explain.

"I'm so sorry. She was getting better and then someone rang the doorbell—"

"Angela, she's not getting better," Jen interrupted. "Your mother is dying."

Fuck you, Jen.

Who says "your mom is dying" all plain like that? Certainly no one in the past six weeks had. Hell, I had to cross that hospital bridge several times before Dr. Fox even put down a guesstimate death date. Even the fancy Hollywood doctor who suggested hospice never said death was certain. I knew from my online toilet searches that a percentage of people "graduate" from hospice and go on to lead normal lives. My mom's friends—many of whom worked in medicine—kept sending her cards ordering her to "get well soon." Why would they tell her to do something they knew she couldn't do?

"But she was walking better than ever earlier. Even cleaning," I argued with Jen.

"That's called rallying. It's usually what happens right before people die," she said, her voice lined with a bit more softness, more patience, which only made me feel more awful. I realized that I was forcing another woman to explain that she knew how to do her job—I've been that woman—but still, Jen's job was death, and I saw mine as the opposite. For her to do her job would mean I'd have to admit I'd failed at my own, so I continued arguing. I broke out my stack of internet-learned facts.

"But I read that 4 percent of people who enter hospice recover and go on to live normal—"

"Most of those people were misdiagnosed. They should have never been in hospice in the first place."

Damn. She got me with that one. I knew statistics never tell the whole story; except when they say there's a 30 percent chance my mom's cancer can be cured, then I believe them wholeheartedly.

"Any final things you need to do with her, you need to do now. She has, at most, a few days."

I nodded, again trying to hold back tears. "Thank you," I said then felt embarrassed for saying it. Who thanks someone for telling them their mom is dying?

Before leaving, Jen told me to call her if I needed anything, but that I probably wouldn't be needing anything as she was upgrading my mom to twenty-four seven care. We'd have nurses in the house full-time, taking over everything from medications to bathing. I was a loser who couldn't even be trusted with a washcloth. After she left, I let my tears flow freely while people in the waiting area glanced away like crying was contagious and they hoped they didn't catch that in addition to whatever sickness had brought them into the ER.

I shook off my tears and walked into my mom's emergency bay. She was alert but her face was blank; there was no more pain, no more confusion, but also no more of the spark I saw in my kitchen. As she lay on that hospital bed, removed from the familiarity of my home, I saw her for the first time, not as my mom but as a woman whose body had completely rebelled against her. Trying to convince that battered body to keep racing for a cure was futile. More than futile, it seemed cruel. Still, knowing a fact and accepting it are two different things entirely. If I accepted her broken body could no longer contain her spirit, what did that mean for me? How could I live without a mother? I felt selfish for thinking about myself.

After the ER doc checked for fractures, he asked if I felt comfortable taking her home in such a state. I had been caring for her in that same state for a week and no one had asked me if I felt competent. I was ashamed, assuming the doctor had read the EMT's notes that my mom was in his care because "neglectful daughter ran out for snacks."

"I can take her home. It's fine," I said, even though I no longer felt anything close to competent.

Once the EMTs drove my mom home and helped me place her back in her bed, she stayed there the rest of the night. Under the watchful eye of a new hospice nurse, I sponge-bathed my mom while she slept. I wondered if she knew I was finally trying to accept what she'd told me before we'd left Philly, that she was dying. I knew I had to be strong and do what I always said I'd do and give her exactly what she needed; however, I was certain I did not contain that much strength. How do you transition from fighting for your mom's life to throwing up your hands and learning to say goodbye? I chose not to think about it, because when I did, I felt like I would completely lose my mind, going over and over in my head how much I failed her and how I'd be without her for the rest of my life because I wasn't enough to save her. I fell asleep on the floor next to her bed, afraid that if I left the room for anything, I'd miss my mom's last breath.

———

When my mother awoke the next morning. I raised a glass of water to her dry lips. She could only take a few sips. She smiled and wished me good morning and told me that she'd left an envelope by my front door.

"What envelope?"

"Before I fell. The guy who rang the doorbell gave it to me," she whispered, her voice tired. She got the rest of her point across by gesturing toward the living room. I'd almost forgotten the doorbell had been the catalyst for her fall. In the living room, I saw a manila envelope by the front door, hand-addressed to me with no postage. I ripped it open. It was a court summons, courtesy of Bill.

Bill was suing me for, among other alleged offenses, "kidnapping" my mom from Philadelphia, emptying her accounts, and for kicking him out of the home he was entitled to in her will. The "other items" were her wedding ring, a dining room table, and a buffalo nickel. Yes, a buffalo nickel. Apparently, the police escort assigned to him when my brother took out the protection order didn't give him enough time to remove the buffalo nickel, et al., so he was suing me, the "rich" television-writer daughter in hopes of a cash settlement for the emotional distress. In twenty-four hours I'd gone from celebratory cheesecake with plans to join a church to being told my mom would be dead in days and her husband was suing me for a nickel.

Perfect timing, I thought. *I needed a new toilet hobby.* Instead of looking up cures on the commode, I now looked up lawyers.

"Guess who made you fall?" I asked my mom. I hoped the "who" portion of the question teased that her trip wire was her husband.

"Hmm? What happened?!" my mom replied, her voice startled as if I'd just interrupted a lucid dream. I had, to be fair, sprung the question on her while her eyes were closed. I needed her to know that her husband had also contributed to her fall. *I'm not a complete moron for leaving the doorbell plugged in! You didn't make a mistake letting me care for you; it was your husband who injured you! And from across the country!*

"That guy who rang the bell? He was delivering a court summons," I said.

"For who?"

"For me."

"From who?"

"From Bill."

"No, he didn't," my mom said, sighing.

"Yes, he did." I sat on the edge of her bed and showed her the summons. "Your husband decided to sue your daughter for kidnapping you and for a damn buffalo nickel."

I had practiced that sentence construction: "Your husband (not my stepdad) decided to sue your daughter (little innocent me whose hair you used to braid) for kidnapping (that's funny but damn, that's also a felony, how dare he) and a buffalo nickel (that's pathetic, your husband was a bum)."

"He bought that nickel from one of those old *Time/Life* magazine collectible commercials," she said. "Old fool thought it would someday be worth thousands."

Mom raised her reading glasses to her nose and flipped through the summons with a look of disbelief, like she was sure to find a big *Psych!* stamped somewhere in its thick pages.

"Don't worry, I got it under control," I continued. "I've already hired a Pennsylvania lawyer since Bill's suing me there," I said, before explaining that the lawyer said we needed to get a new will in order, pronto.

I'd let the lawyer and his wants lead that sentence, leaving me far from the dirty task of bringing up uncomfortable topics related to death such as wills and last wishes. I expected my mom to apologize on Bill's behalf, like she did after he was arrested. Instead, she let out a giggle while she adjusted the hospital bed to an upright position. She was suddenly fully awake.

"I hope he knows he's suing you for a house he can't afford payments on. He probably thinks it's paid off," she said, letting out another laugh. "If that man paid one bill, then he'd know the house is underwater," she continued. "Well, I guess he'll know after we fill out this will, won't he? I bought my own wedding ring, by the way. He can't have it," she said.

I handed Mom the simple will my lawyer had suggested and retreated back to my corner of the room. I didn't want to seem like I was staring over her shoulder as she decided which loved ones got which assets. When she handed the completed paper back to me, I tried to be a dignified executrix and not say *What the fuck, Mom?* after seeing that she'd allotted 10 percent to Bill.

"Bill wasn't all terrible," she said cautiously. I tried to conceal my hurt even though I knew his 10 percent was literally 10 percent of zero. I knew how much nothing she had because as power of attorney, I paid her bills. The only money she had was her yet-to-be-received disability check.

"If that's what you want, that's what he'll get. I promise," I said, stunned and a bit pissed by her capacity to perceive goodness in someone who was suing her daughter. While she slept, I often thought of how many years of my own life I'd give up to punch Bill in the face once (ten years, twelve if I could break his nose). I tried to shift to happier thoughts, to be grateful I, not Bill, was with my mother in her last moments. In the two weeks she'd been at my home, we were finally doing everything we were too busy working to ever do: We were simply being together, sitting, talking, listening, relaxing. I hoped cramming these moments in at the end of her life would make up for all those years I only visited at Christmas. As I tried to remember what a gift it was to be with her in her last moments, I settled on at least admitting it was better than receiving a call from Bill after she'd already passed.

"Bill does not know who he's fighting," my mom told me with

a knowing smile before falling asleep again. Perhaps she knew my anger would take care of his karma.

I texted my brother: The hospice nurse said mom has two days at most! Get on a flight now!!

I sat back on the floor with my phone and leveled up in a video game. That dopamine hit felt better than the emotions that creeped in when I thought that in days, I'd have no mother to watch while she slept. I was trying my best to not be a selfish, hoarding child and accept that, to her, the peacefulness of death was preferable to the pain of life in a body that had already given up. I tried to reckon with the fact that necessary things can also be terrible things as I prepared to give her a good death, just as I'd tried to give her everything else she'd asked for.

9

New Notebook and Acceptance

May 28: Pt awake and alert. Lethargic. Respiration even and unlabored. Pain is controlled. Maintain safe and hazard-free environment. Skin is dusky edema. Voiding small amounts. Bilateral upper extremities.

Maintain safe and hazard-free environment. Did the nurses really have to write that and rub it in? After I let my mom slip on her own pants, that part should be a given, like "make sure patient still has skin before inserting needle." If the nurses thought I was a dunce, I wanted to make sure they knew *she* wasn't so I hung her prized hospital ID around her bedpost: Gwen Nissel, RN, BSN. She grinned at it when she woke up. I hoped it made her feel less vulnerable. I only left her side to pee. While she slept, I answered all her phone calls and finally admitted that she was in hospice. I regretted making a big deal of her rallying, because, of course, her being in hospice came as a shock to most people who called. I tried my best to soothe her friends.

"She's resting. Like *resting*, resting," I said.

"I swear, I really tried. Even the LA doctor had nothing."

"Well, no, I don't think the plane ride put her into hospice," I said to my mom's neighbor and lamented that just like me, everyone thinks they're a doctor at the absolute worst times.

After multiple phone calls, the afternoon nurse, Jade, pulled me from my mother's bedside and toward the kitchen. Jade was my favorite nurse, if only because she smiled at my mom's RN ID and greeted her as "Nurse Gwen." Once in the kitchen, Jade's usual whisper voice took on a stern edge.

"Even if she's sleeping, she can hear everything you say. Hearing is the last sense to go so any uncomfortable phone calls you need to make should be made outside her room. Your job now is just to be her daughter and help her have a good death."

That should have been a relief—I didn't have to *do* anything. But inwardly I got defensive because I wasn't used to being chastised by a near stranger in my own home. If my mom was prepared to die, how could it make her uncomfortable to hear that she was indeed dying? Was it because she would worry about how it would affect me? I realized I had no idea what a good death was beyond being by someone's side.

Jade and the other hospice nurses seemed able to immediately gauge my mom's needs from even the slightest facial expressions. If her eyebrows rose, that meant the pain had broken through and she needed morphine. A slightly scrunched-up face, like she'd eaten something tart, meant her diaper needed changing. Later that same day, Jade somehow also knew that diapers were no longer enough and that my mom needed a catheter.

"I don't want a catheter," Mom told her, looking up at me from her bed for backup.

I pulled Jade into the kitchen. "If she doesn't want a catheter, she's not getting one," I said, certain that in standing up for my mom, I was doing my assigned job of just being her daughter.

"She needs a catheter. She doesn't want one because she's a nurse and she knows what it means," Jade explained.

Once again, I was ignorant. I didn't know what it meant—or how it could be worse than having one in your chest. I also didn't want to know, so I didn't ask. I didn't understand why my mom couldn't just rest while waiting for death. Wasn't the point of accepting death to stop all the medical interventions she didn't want? Still, I was proud I didn't even sit on the toilet searching the internet for catheter alternatives. When I did take my next break to sit on the toilet, I prayed that my mom's last words wouldn't be "I don't want a catheter," especially when I couldn't fulfill that request. I had no idea what to do as "just a daughter." I felt helpless. Then I thought of how much she loved when I sent her flowers for Mother's Day. I picked flowers from my yard and put them in a vase next to her bed and hoped that counted for something.

———

May 29: Received pt in bed. Agitated and confused. Respiration fast and labored. Requested more pain medication. Assisted family in music therapy.

My mom's agitation and confusion were due, in part, to being woken up by a music therapy volunteer on a guitar.

"Is that white girl singing a song from *The Wizard of Oz*?" Mom asked, after calling me over to her side so only I could hear her whispered question. She glanced over at the young woman suspiciously as she strummed "Somewhere Over the Rainbow."

"She's Gretchen. A volunteer," I said.

Mom dropped her confused face and suddenly beamed that someone had come to sing just for her. "Thank you, Gretchen," she said.

My mom's ability to speak was something I no longer took for granted. She was down to only a handful of sentences a day. When she spoke, I always tried to passively get a few more out of her by telling her I loved her. If her eyes were open, she'd always find just enough strength to reply.

"I love you too," she'd say before she settled back down and closed her eyes. If "I love you" would be the last words she spoke, I could deal. As I walked Gretchen to the door, I wondered if she had lost someone too. I wanted to feel like Gretchen acted. Like losing a mom isn't scary. Like you can sing when a life is ending because you know important things like hearing being the last sense to go. When Gretchen left, I read Maya Angelou to my mother. As I did, I no longer cared about my mom's last words. I only cared about saying words I wanted her to hear. I sat by her side reading *Phenomenal Woman* until the sun went down.

"Phenomenal woman. You know that's what you are right, Mom?"

10

Brothers and Flowers

My brother arrived and claimed the only free corner of the bedroom as his sitting vigil space. Like me, he sat on the floor, facing Mom's bed. With four people in the room and two dogs, it was crowded, and Jack and I had to step over each other to use the bathroom. My mom's dogs seemed to think we were sitting on the floor because it was playtime. They happily scampered around from my brother's lap to mine, rolling on their backs for belly scratches. I was jealous of their ignorance.

With no TV in the room, we'd sit for hours, just petting the dogs and listening to spring sounds come through the open windows. At times, my mom's labored breathing was the loudest sound in the room. I stepped over my brother to pick more flowers from my garden; this time I placed one behind Mom's ear. Her eyes stayed closed, but her lips pursed into the slightest of smiles as she felt my fingers tuck the stem into her hair.

It had become crystal clear that my mom was more than her physical body. Over the days, I had watched that body lose many of the functions we consider "life" but her spirit was still tangibly there. It was a presence that couldn't be diminished; she often seemed more "there" than when she could still stand up or open her eyes. Or perhaps, in the quiet of the room and attempting to "just be" her daughter, I paid more attention to her spirit. Sitting on the floor, I was certain of very little, but I knew those moments of love as she used her last bit of energy to smile at flowers and the touch of my hand were as important as anything happening on the planet. Death transformed from being my sworn enemy to being the only force that could give Mom's spirit the comfort it deserved. Saying that aloud would sound like I wished my mom was dead, so I never did.

After we watched her smile fade, Jack and I took a quick break in the kitchen. It was the place we went to talk and curse outside of my mom's earshot.

"Shit, this is beautiful and fucked-up at the same time," my brother said.

"Yeah. Shit, man," I said, agreeing to what we both didn't know how to put into words.

———

May 30: Give morphine every two hours. Family in agreement.

———

May 31: Pitting edema in all extremities. Pt has difficulty swallowing liquids. Pleural cavity drained.

I didn't know (and still don't know) what pitting edema is. I no longer had the need to look up every complicated medical word I didn't understand. The words the nurses wrote didn't reflect the small miracles that seemed to happen the more time ticked on. Yes, "Pt has difficulty swallowing liquids" was a sign that my mom had almost reached the end, but it was also one of the first times in my life she let me help her without arguing that I was fussing over her. I'd wet a washcloth and hold it to her lips, watching her face relax as the moisture hit her tongue. I repeated over and over how much I appreciated and loved her. Usually my "I love yous" didn't have much emotion behind them; they were words I tossed off, by rote, at the end of our long-distance catch-up calls. Now, every time I got to say those words, it felt like a tremendous gift that I could and that she could still hear me. If it's true that hearing is the last sense to go, then she also heard my brother and I play a game of who could find the earliest memory to thank her for. My brother thanked her for not killing him when, at four, he brought a sprinkler inside the house to cool off the TV. In between the spoken love, I started thinking about how much I took for granted, like the feel of water on my lips and the touch of loved ones. Despite what Mom would call my California hippie side, I was also grateful for the lab-made morphine that soothed her pain.

Even with the high dosage of miracle morphine that kept her asleep most of the day, that morning, my mom's eyes shot open from a deep slumber and followed an unseen person around the room.

"Who is that?" she asked. Her suddenly open eyes didn't hold fear, just curiosity, like she'd spotted someone waving to her and she couldn't place the face. Whoever my mom was seeing was as real to her as I was.

"Who are *they*?" Mom continued, as if whoever was in the room had suddenly invited more people along. This time her voice was more politely concerned, like she was improperly dressed for whatever party was about to start in her bedroom. As her eyes scanned the unseen people, our crowded room felt a bit brighter, joyful even, much like it does when you're in the presence of a friend who "lights up a room." Whoever these friends visiting my mom were, they carried warmth, they were welcoming, and apparently had brought her gifts.

"They brought me roses," she said, her eyes crinkling into a smile.

I'd been filling up time by reading what happens when someone is actively dying, and it was as helpful as speed-reading *What to Expect While You're Expecting* when you're already on the delivery table. But still, I did gather from that speed-read that hospice patients often "hallucinated" about taking a trip or seeing loved ones. From someone very experienced with people hallucinating (once again, shout-out to the psych ward), this didn't feel like a hallucination. The nurse didn't call for backup or grab for an injection of a sedative. She looked as if she'd seen this before and it was as normal to her as the catheters and painkillers. She smiled at my mom.

"They bought you roses, huh? Sounds like people are excited to see you," she said.

"It's all the mothers and babies you helped at the hospital," I said, guessing as to who would be in such a large heavenly welcoming crowd like the one in the corner of the room, then hating that I'd stupidly suggested that all the patients my mom helped were dead. Still, she nodded as if she trusted me and closed her eyes again, still smiling at the roses only she could see.

—

June 1: Assisted with positioning. Patient remains uncomfortable with uncontrolled symptoms. Assisted with repositioning.

If I'd read the above notes before we signed up for hospice, I probably would have kidnapped my mom from it just as Bill had suggested I'd already done. "Uncontrolled symptoms" to me reads like my mom was thrashing in pain, as if she was fighting off death like a gravely injured movie action hero. Instead, her uncomfortableness manifested in small signs, like a furrowed brow or a soft hum.

I thought about how the pain of bringing my brother and me into the world seemed worse than the pain she was experiencing leaving it. From what our mom shared about our births, there was plenty of screaming, gripping of blankets, and begging for epidurals. Most moments waiting for death were calm. As my brother and I stayed by her side still learning how to "just be" her children, I wondered if, like hearing, Mom's smell was still intact. I laughed inside thinking how embarrassed she'd be if she could smell her children's rank, unwashed asses. We both refused to leave her side to shower.

Jack and I took turns doing things that don't stop for death, like letting the dogs out. Byron usually covered mundane chores like this, but when he was at work, instead of walking downstairs to the backyard—too far from Mom—we'd let the dogs out on the un-fenced front lawn. It usually worked out as long as we kept a watchful eye out for squirrels or other dogs. *Usually.* This day I hadn't looked through the peephole before opening the door and my dog, Woody, charged after a cute poodle who was peeing on my plants. I grabbed him before he could make the poodle his meal.

"I'm so sorry—"

"Jesus! He almost bit my dog!" the woman said and scooped up her poodle, glaring at me in my two-day-old clothes as I grabbed Woody's collar and led him back into the house.

"Again, I'm so, so sorry," I continued, but the expression on her face read that this was the absolute worst thing to happen to her that day and she wouldn't be right until I got on my knees and begged for forgiveness.

"I could report you!"

"Fuck it, report me then. My mom is dying. Sorry I made *your* day so bad," I said, shutting the door in her face, wondering why God still let life keep going when my emotional plate was full. To one of my neighbors, I am now the funky-smelling lady with an aggressive dog who invokes her dying mom to avoid responsibility. If my mom wasn't actively dying, I would have stayed on my lawn making amends for the dog bite that did not happen, but now, I refused to waste time on dumb shit, given how little time my mom had left.

"Did something happen outside?" Nurse Jade asked.

"Nope, all good."

I sat back down and read a few more Maya Angelou verses. When I was done, Jade stroked my mom's hair.

"You sure are hanging in there," Jade said to Mom, then motioned me into the living room. Once we were out of her earshot, Jade's voice took on the same stern tone it had when she had warned me about Mom hearing my phone calls.

"Sometimes people like to pass away alone," she said. I took this to mean that hovering over our mom twenty-four seven does not make for a good death. But, unlike with the catheter, I didn't give in to Jade's opinion. I was staying in that room until Mom woke up and told me herself to leave. She didn't. So I stayed. And invited more people.

I thought it would help Mom pass if she knew I had friends who would take care of me once she was gone. During the week, my friends stopped by, most of them meeting her for the first time. As my mom slept, I walked her through who my friends were.

"This is Joy, the woman who took a chance on me and got me my first writing job," I said, while hoping God hadn't already told Mom I was jobless. If he had, I knew she would never take her last breath until Joy got me another job. She met Nicole, who had ten years on me and was, like my mom was at her job, one of the women who had often cornered me in bathrooms to keep me from burning our former workplace down. The last friend brought her toddler and Mom blinked her eyes open for the first time in over twenty-four hours as the little girl sat on her bed. I gave myself dap for my choice of "mothers and babies" as the answer to who Mom was seeing in the corner. Despite meeting my friends, my mom still refused to pass. I used caffeine and phone games to stay awake, afraid she'd choose to leave when I was sleeping. My online team gave me kudos, asking how I completed so many game levels in a day.

A chaplain stopped by and asked if he could read the Bible to my mom.

"I'd love that," I said, and if my mom's hearing was truly still working, I was surprised she didn't at least flutter her eyes at my response like she did at the toddler. At sixteen, I'd explained to her in a "know-it-all" voice that I was breaking our family curse of praying to gods that were forced on our ancestors. A photo of one of those ancestors, Aunt Hattie, was now next to Mom's bed. I'd taken it from my shelf and placed it next to her Bible. Aunt Hattie had only one eye and, postemancipation, lived in North Carolina across from the KKK headquarters. "Apparently, you'd visit her house and you'd see her rifle before you saw her yellow head," my uncle once said. As the chaplain read to my mom, I silently asked both Aunt Hattie and God to watch over her, figuring that it wouldn't be a bad thing to also have an ancestor with a shotgun on your side as you crossed over.

The chaplain asked to speak to me privately. He asked if I had any questions. I said I was tired of questions that had no answers. For example, why was Death taking his sweet time now that we'd accepted his invitation? As I watched Mom's breaths become more labored that day, I wondered if Jade was correct and my mom wanted to be alone. But I also knew that was a mother-daughter spat I was determined to win, so I pushed that thought away and drank more caffeine to stay awake.

June 2: Pain unable to manage with 20 mg morphine 2 hrs
PRN. New order. Sbl patch will send tomorrow to avoid over-
dosing of morphine.

Don't ask me what a Sbl patch is. All I know is the nurse ordered
it once my mom's throat made a whistling noise with each inhaled
breath. The nurse called it a death rattle. *Death*, apparently, was no
longer a taboo word once it was this close.

"The death rattle doesn't mean she's in pain. It just means other
parts of her body are shutting down," she assured me. "She's ready
to go," she added in a way that, again, hinted that my brother and I
needed to scram. My brother and I stayed, continuing to talk to our
mom about memories.

"You remember when we fought with hot sauce?" my brother
asked her.

We were now digging into the deep cuts end of the memory
pool, reminding her of things she probably would rather forget, like
having to take a day off from work when she found me with hot
sauce burning my retina after my brother and I'd had a food fight.

My mom continued rattling and defiantly hanging on.

Jade pulled me into the kitchen again. "I really think she's waiting for you to leave the room. Sometimes parents don't want to burden kids with seeing them pass away."

I nodded as if taking her words to heart, but I was thinking,
*Damn, even in her last moments my mom wants to protect me from
what she thinks is a burden. We are in a literal fight until the death
over her own death.* Again, I ignored Jade and I vowed to stay in the
fight. I borrowed another of my mom's favorite sayings: My house,

my rules. The newly implemented rule of my house was: If you die here, I will be by your side.

"Mom, it's okay. You can go if you're ready. I'm going to stay right with you."

She kept on breathing, like she was stubbornly determined to hold on longer than I could.

———

June 3: Pt in transition. Maintain pt comfort.

My brother and I stood over Mom as she slept, just like we did when we were kids and ignored her pleas for "just a little more rest." Every time she furrowed her brow, we shot looks at each other: *She's giving in, she wants us here.* Still, she kept hanging on. It was the death version of two kids in the back seat continually asking "Are we there yet?" Our mom probably wished she couldn't hear.

"Wanna get some air?" my brother asked. Both my brother and I needed a break from the all-night heavenly tug-of-war.

We stood by the front door, sharing a cigarette, something we hadn't done since our rebellious teen years, when we had graduated from fighting with hot sauce to sharing forties of beer. We wordlessly puffed smoke across the steps that had brought our mom down and the bushes that grew the flowers now in her hair. I looked down and saw a dead bee and thought, *Are there always so many dead bees or is this the first time I've taken the time to sit on my front steps and notice?* And then I puffed out more smoke and potentially killed another one.

The cigarette ash almost to the filter, my brother took a final puff and stomped the embers out under his slipper. As we reentered the house to take our usual spots on the floor, Jade blocked our way to the bedroom.

"She's leaving," Jade whispered, her arms stretched across the door's threshold to guard my mom's privacy. I raised Jade's arm above her head and held it up like a drawbridge while my brother and I passed under it. We both kneeled on opposite sides of our mom, taking each of her hands in one of ours.

"It's okay. We're okay," I said.

"You can go now. We'll be fine," my brother said, smiling at Mom. Her face scrunched up. She took another labored breath. Then another. I imagined Jade looking at me disapprovingly like my old babysitters. *Child, if you don't let your mom be . . .*

"This is your room forever, Mom. You can haunt it," I said. Because I wondered if she was scared and I knew a joke would make her feel more at ease.

"You taught us how to be good people, we'll take care of each other," Jack said. He reached out for my free hand so all of us were joined together. My mom's whistling breaths came in spurts with a long pause between each one. It was as if each one took considerable effort, but effort she was willing to give. We had to let her know she didn't need to try so hard anymore, that we would look out for each other just like she'd always done for us.

"You go relax in heaven. It's pretty over there," I said and that was not one of my lies. I was certain of that, that where she was going was prettier than what she'd been through. A single tear welled up in her eyes and fell down her cheek. The next whistling breath we were waiting for never came.

"She's gone," Jade quietly announced, and I turned, having forgotten Jade was even in the room. Her face was streaked with tears she didn't try to wipe away. And I thought, *She does this every day and she's crying. We must have given Mom a good death.* With the single tear still staining her cheek, my brother and I kissed our mom one final time. I would hold on to that tear; it taught me that words don't need to be spoken for them to be heard. That tear contained everything left unsaid. It meant our mom loved us more than we could ever imagine and that she was proud of us, we'd done well. As we left Jade to prepare the body, I didn't cling to it or ask her to give me a moment. The body on the bed was no longer Mom, it was clearly just a beaten-up shell. Just like she was proud of us, I was proud of her for finally leaving pain behind to find freedom, and grateful that she let me "just be" my usual hardheaded pain in the ass while she did.

11

Grief Chores

am positively certain that I gave my mom the best death I could give. If I have to die one day, I want to go exactly like she did, surrounded by loved ones and a competent nurse in case my loved ones are like me and have no idea what the hell they're doing. When times get tough, I still find comfort in the single grateful tear that slid down Mom's cheek and the pure, unspoken love my brother and I surrounded her with in her final hours. However, within one day of her passing, that pure love transformed into pure hate. Toward a teen girl. More specifically, toward a teen girl in an ad. She was a block from my house, her big blond billboard-size head smiling down on me because she'd beaten cancer.

The billboard was captioned: *Resilience. Pass it on.*

Pass this on: Fuck you, I thought.

The billboard seemed to be taunting me. Apparently that teen deserved to live and my mom didn't. *Why couldn't I have found a way to make my mom resilient like that young blond girl?*

Once I started asking questions like that, other questions would see their opening and jump up, demanding their own answers:

Did my agreeing to more morphine kill her? Could I have at least gotten those six months the doctor wrote on her disability form if I hadn't signed up with hospice? Maybe the flight did kill her? If only my broke ass could afford first class. Why couldn't I, finally, at the end, be a gotdamn better daughter? A better daughter could have saved her life. I forced myself to push those thoughts away, because thinking too long about them made me certain I'd never feel normal again. I'd stop being mad at myself only to get mad at my mom for leaving me. Then I'd get mad at myself for being mad at a dead mom. Some days I'd just lie in bed and wish I could die too.

My mom was fucking dead. No dancing around it with euphemisms now. She was gone, and now I could say words like *fucking* out loud whenever I pleased because no one would be disappointed in me. And that was a scary-ass feeling. I didn't feel old enough to not have a mom, but I also felt like a loser for being grown yet still wanting mine so badly. It felt like the floor had fallen out from under me. Just my floor. All other floors all around the world were solidly intact.

If I managed to pull myself out of my pajamas to go outside, I'd see women around my mom's age doing normal things and thought, *Why can't my mom do normal things anymore?* Even a sixty-something buying soup made me jealous and indignant on Mom's behalf. *My mom doesn't get to buy soup!* When I wasn't consumed by anger, every single part of my life felt cloudy in a way that, for me, felt worse than severe depression. Those clouds covering everything had a concrete reason I could point to and no one could argue it was all in my chemically imbalanced head. It was like everyone in the world could choose to be happy and normal, but in my life, those options were grayed out.

The one thing I wasn't mad at was cancer. It had one job—to destroy—and cancer had done that job well. If cancer were a co-worker, my mom would have been envious of how hard it worked. I still never said "Fuck Cancer" but instead, I said fuck billboards and pink license plate frames and sugar-filled pink yogurt cups and anything else that ever made me believe that cancer could be beaten with positive buzzwords. And especially fuck whoever in my thirty-five years of life had never mentioned that being in charge of a loved one's estate while deep in grief was a job that I might want to outsource.

When I agreed to be Mom's executrix, I agreed because, well, in those last days, for anything she wanted, I tried to reply with yes. I was hoping she'd shed her church girl vibe and want something fun like street drugs. I had no idea where I'd get them, but if she had wanted some cocaine, I would have sold my soul to make it happen and stayed up partying with her all night. But cheesecake and me being the executrix were as much as my selfless mom wanted. Plus, I thought "executrix settling the estate" sounded like a fancy job, like a lady with a parasol figuring how to level her mansion lawn. The post-death online guides made it sound like a gift to be chosen as an executrix; it meant my mom thought I was honest, responsible, and financially savvy. I'd argue those guides left important details out. Instead of choosing the honest, fiscally responsible person in my family, I am going to choose someone I secretly barely like. Someone I want to make figure out how to get certified copies of my death certificates over and over. Someone who I want to experience the hell of telling credit card AI service representatives that I died. I'd wait on hold for twenty minutes, then be unable to speak to a human customer service representative because the last hold song brought me to tears. How dare Stevie Wonder call someone to say he loved them, doesn't he know I can't call my mom anymore?

Being an executrix is the worst volunteer job ever. Even doing the job I'd accepted out of love made me angry. It was combining the two aspects of myself I hated the most, having a dead mom and my failure to thrive under capitalism.

There were dozens of financial tasks to do and, unlike my mom choosing when she'd take her last breath, those tasks had strict legal deadlines. Moments after the van pulled off with my mom's body inside, I started on executrix chores and their sister chore: calling every damn body your loved one has ever known and telling them she died.

Unlike the physical task of caring for my mom, no hospice worker could help with this. My boyfriend, Byron, couldn't be the silent aide in the background. My brother had to go home and I was mad about that because him leaving reminded me that he had what I no longer had, family members to live with and care for. I was completely alone calling a long list of my mom's friends repeating over and over that she'd passed. I put on a strong face and pushed down all my feelings to calmly deliver the when, where, and hows of her death and to agree by rote, that yes, I knew she was still looking down at me. Sometimes her friends would cry. When they did, I added them to the list of people I temporarily hated, wondering why I had to carry her friends' grief when I didn't even know how to carry my own. When they'd cry, I'd rush off the phone pretending I had another death chore to attend to; when they didn't cry, I'd still use death chores as an excuse to rush off the phone because none of them were clairvoyant and could figure out I was lying.

I wanted them to be clairvoyant. I desperately wanted one of her friends to sense that my claims of being okay were lies and the real answer to their "How are yous?" was "I'm jealous of my mom. Death seems like a great option right now. If only she hadn't left her dogs behind to force me to stay alive." *Great trick, Mom. That's why you bought your dogs here, huh?*

My brother was my only respite from hiding my anger and being on my best death chore behavior. We'd text each other with questions and complaints as after two days of straight dialing, I still hadn't made it through Mom's four-page friend list. I texted him almost every hour and often broke out into panic attacks that he had died if I didn't get a response within minutes.

> **Me:** Who is Mrs. Raina?
>
> **Jack:** She was the babysitter who made us eat day-old rye bread while her kids got the fresh white shit.
>
> **Me:** Our babysitter? Why is she crying like she just lost her only kidney donor?
>
> **Jack:** Right? We hated her! Why did Mom put her on the list of people to call?
>
> **Me:** Repeating "my mom passed" over and over fucking sucks. I'm just going to group text everyone a skull and cross-bones emoji.
>
> **Jack:** You know Mom raised you better than that. At least send individual texts.

After I finally finished her friend list and beat myself up over death etiquette (Is it okay to leave a voicemail about your mom dying?), I continued calling every bank that ever appeared on her credit report. I broke out into tears when a customer service agent walked me through closing the bank accounts my mom and I had only opened last month. Barbara from the Benefits Office seemed surprised when I called her directly to discuss my mom's disability check. She told me someone had already called to see if it could be forwarded to him. She couldn't give a name, just "someone."

> **Me:** Did you call Mom's Benefits Office?
> **Jack:** No.
> **Me:** Bill did. That mofo is trying to find more money!
> **Jack:** He knows she ain't have none bc if she did, we'd use it to buy a slicer to cut off his hands like they did in the Bible.
> **Me:** Slice 'em right off!

I was mad that in the millions of years people have been dying, no one had invented a magic button you can press to inform every utility and credit card that your mom is dead and needs to cancel. When I'd press a number to cancel, I was usually transferred to a live customer service representative.

"I see you're calling to cancel, Ms. Gwen Nissel. Can I entice you to stay with three months free?" said a customer service rep from my mom's internet provider.

"Gwen is my mom. I'm her daughter. I promise you she really no longer needs internet, not even for three months free."

"You sure there's not anything we can do to keep her?"

"She's dead, so no."

"I'm so sorry. I'll go ahead and cancel."

After a few days, the calls felt like telephone torture. I'm not a fan of talking on the phone, even in nongrief times. To get me through how many times I had to say "My mom is dead," I decided to keep a spreadsheet of how much she'd saved by dying. It always made me forget my anger for a few seconds. We loved a bargain and technically, my mom had gotten the last month of every utility and her mortgage payment for free. She had more than $35,000 of "free" on the credit cards alone! Then I remembered I was the one who had to fly to Philly and clean out that $35,000 worth of stuff so we could sell her underwater house. I also had to plan a Philly memorial. During almost every call I made to my mom's friends, one of them reminded me of that by asking me when the memorial was going to be. I'd always reply that I did not know.

> **Me:** I'm not planning a fucking Philly memorial service!
>
> **Jack:** Neither the fuck am I.
>
> **Me:** Then tell everyone asking me about the damn memorial to plan it themselves!! Mom wanted a SIMPLE memorial!!! Her will says BURIED AT SEA!!! Philly don't have seas! I am picking up her ashes and giving her that exact wish in California!!!
>
> **Jack:** I'll tell them, greedy memorial-wanting bastards.

I checked off another death chore by picking up my mom's ashes, mad that the salesman tried to finagle me into upgrading my mom's urn. The next day, I headed to the beach to spread those ashes with

Candi and Belle in tow. I wanted her dogs to see a part of California my mom would never get to experience. I had planned to take her to the ocean as soon as she healed. We'd celebrate by taking another photo of her barely in the water like we did in Antigua.

I'd carefully planned out an early morning beach trip so the afternoon's hot sand wouldn't burn her pups' paws. We walked and her pups stayed by my side as I held the urn steady and trudged across the sand. I plotted a path to the ocean that avoided any part of the beach with kids. I didn't want a mom to have to explain to Little Timmy that my own mom was in that funny-shaped vase and soon she would be part of his sandcastle. As we continued walking, Mom's dogs heard their first loud wave crash to shore and their inner-city asses both froze and peed, like it was the scariest shit they ever heard. I felt horrible, immediately U-turned and put all three of us back in the car. I put my mom's urn in the trunk after working out what would be more disrespectful—me putting her urn in the trunk or her dogs accidentally opening and playing with the ashes on the hour drive back home. Arriving home, I opened the urn for the first time and saw my mom's ashes were in a Ziploc bag. That made me angrier. I wondered if it was because I'd bought the basic brass urn that my mom got placed in a Ziploc bag someone else would have used for Cheez-Its.

I returned to the beach the next day without the dogs or the urn, just the Ziploc bag. I crossed the sand determined to give my mom her final wish of burial at sea. The Ziploc bag was easier to carry than the urn, but it had its own challenges. I discovered that carrying a Ziploc bag full of dark gray ashes made people suspicious that I was dumping trash in the ocean. Some of the senior beach walkers seemed to be giving me side-eye as they power walked past me and the bag. After briefly hating them because they were older than my mom but alive and walking on a beach like she was supposed to be doing, I realized I *was* essentially dumping trash in the ocean. They were ashes. I wouldn't want to swim in someone else's mom's ashes. I slipped into more self-consciousness than I had with the urn. I googled some prayers to say for burials at sea, figuring those would make the act of dumping about ninety cigarettes' worth of ashes feel a bit more holy. The first result was how flinging mom ashes into the ocean from the sand is illegal: Human remains must be scattered at least three nautical miles from shore.

Of course, I was then mad I had spent two days in cross-town traffic, traumatized her dogs, and couldn't get one final simple buried-at-sea memorial request done. I struggled back through the sand, then across the asphalt parking lot, still determined to not give in to the pressure of having to plan a memorial all the way in Philadelphia.

> **Me:** I tried to bury Mom at sea, but it's illegal. I'm going to have a memorial, but not in Philly! Tell everyone in Philly she was strong enough to fly to LA w stage 4 cancer so unless they have that, they can fly their healthy asses out here to her memorial.
>
> **Jack:** Truth!!!
>
> **Me:** Right? We don't need to make them happy by having a memorial in Philly. I can find a church in Los Angeles!

I was mad I couldn't be like my mom and care what her co-workers and friends thought enough to get myself together to plan a

Philly memorial. I felt caught between knowing how much she cared about others' opinions of her and also knowing I didn't have the emotional ability to lose a mom, constantly tell customer service strangers that she was dead, then fly back home and face her crying friends. If even talking to them on the phone broke me down for hours, how was I going to handle hours of it in person? By having the memorial at my house, I was once again hoping to telegraph to them that I was not okay, plus let them know I wasn't 100 percent the letdown of a daughter I'd felt I was: I was having a memorial, just not where they wanted it.

Jack: People have been asking me about her homegoing service. I told them it will be in Los Angeles.

Me: TY. I hate everyone who isn't you and these dogs! And my nephew!

Jack: Like Mom would say, family is the most important thing.

Me: She said that, then she died! Make it make sense!

Jack: It doesn't.

Me: Someone else just bothered me about a Philly memorial and I texted her your number, so you can set her straight.

Jack: I'll handle it.

Me: TY. Damn, I love you, man.

Jack: Love you, too, sis.

Me: Mom is proud. We're taking care of each other.

Jack: You hanging in there? I love you.

Me: Honestly, no. I fucking hate being in this house all alone again. I don't even like Byron being here. I told Mom this was our family house and now I'm planning a memorial for her in it.

Jack: I know. I can only get out of bed because my son needs me. And because Bill's pigeons need their shit cleaned every day.

Me: Fuck everyone else who doesn't understand our pain. Only person we gotta make happy is Mom.

Jack: Amen.

Text-bonding with my brother about how greedy everyone else was became the only death chore I looked forward to. I decided I needed more than the texts. I needed him to move in with me. That the only possible way we could be sure we were taking care of each other—our last promise to our mother as we held her dying hand— was for us to physically be together helping each other through grief.

Me: Mom would want you to move out here. You have to move to Los Angeles.

Jack: I think Mom would want that too.

Me: Right? We told Mom we'd take care of each other, so we gotta do it!

Jack: I'm in.

Me: I don't know what I would do if I didn't have you.

Jack: Back at you. I'm telling the wife we're moving. Go plan your memorial. Mom's friends will deal.

12

Cycle for Mom's Life

For the most part, Mom's friends did not deal. Even though my brother held off as many of them as he could, a few people a day would ring my phone. They'd always start the conversation by checking on how I was holding up—I'd tell them I was fine—they'd then segue into politely asking if they missed a memorial announcement. In what I called self-care, I stopped answering their calls. That was not a smart thing to do, as someone then called a police wellness check on me. I went back to answering the phone.

My aunt Jeanette was one of the many people who phoned me, checking if she'd missed a Philadelphia memorial announcement. Aunt Jeanette was the type of aunt who would plan backyard tea parties, infuse them with proper etiquette, and even buy real scones to have with our tea. She's an emotional carbon copy of my mom; it's like they were born with the same moral DNA. Both my aunt and my mom were women who always remembered thank-you notes and greeting cards; they always had candy in their purse for both well-behaved children and any friends who might go into diabetic shock. They were women who would never outright say you were making a wrong choice but would dance around the edges of your horrible choice in disappointed tones.

"I mean, *most people* would *probably* have a memorial for their mom in the city she lived in," my aunt said after I informed her of my Los Angeles memorial plans. I said nothing. If Aunt Jeanette wanted a Philadelphia memorial, she would have to tell me *how* to do it. I mean, I literally wanted her to tell me how she and my mother gathered so much emotional strength to do shit they didn't want to do just for etiquette and perhaps Jesus's sake. I told my aunt to politely leave me alone, that I would find a nice memorial church in Los Angeles. I didn't even try to call a church. I felt nervous cold-calling churches for a memorial. It seemed rude.

Hi, neither I nor my mom ever went to your church, but we'd like to host her last party there.

Instead of testing out a few churches each Sunday, I continued to get my gospel from the gym. The endorphins from a spin class were a much-needed ritual to keep me on the better side of that depression line. It was also a place where no one asked me to do anything I didn't know how to do, like plan memorials. Instead, the spin instructors shouted encouraging motivation at me. I needed that.

"Get those legs pumping," Chuck, my spin cycle instructor, shouted. "You've done tougher things than this hill!"

He's right! I watched my mom die; there's no reason I can't whip this hill's ass! I'd look around the spin class thinking how I was the toughest in the room and at the very least, if I had to feel so angry and disconnected from every other human being, I was going to have the best legs out of all those bitches. Chuck's class became my sanctuary. So, as one does while riding an endorphin high, I hopped off my bike and asked Chuck to lead my mom's Los Angeles memorial. Unlike any church I cold-called, at least Chuck *knew* my mom.

Perhaps I'm being a tad generous with the definition of the word *knew*; Chuck had been one in that small parade of friends who'd met my mom during her last days. During the twenty minutes Chuck spent with her, Mom was half asleep and seemed only slightly aware that a buff man in a Pride shirt and bike shorts had just gifted her a plant. In my defense, Chuck wasn't only my spin cycle instructor. In the same way everyone at my mom's job knew her, everyone Black at my gym also knew one another. Chuck and I bonded on our bikes because most of the Black members crammed into his first couple classes to welcome him, giving his classes more of a nightclub vibe than the sporty suburban mom aesthetic the spin room normally had. Once I'd stopped pop-locking while screaming "Hoooooo!" at Chuck from a stationary bike, we further bonded; he was a member of the "spiritual but not religious" center I irregularly attended. The one I'd once tricked my mom into attending when she'd visited me. She was obviously suspicious that my church wasn't like hers when she eyed the United Nations mix of people lingering around the "church" entrance.

"I read that cults are the only places where people of all races worship together," my mom said. I reassured her that California churches were different, then she walked in with her fancy sequin church hat only to realize that most worshippers were in jeans. She gasped as a man with long locks introduced himself as a reverend before reading from *Chicken Soup for the Soul*. I stared straight ahead, hoping the side of my face emoted that all California Christian preachers get their gospel from mass-market paperbacks. My mom white-knuckled it through the rest of the service. Near the end, when new visitors were asked to stand, she stayed glued to the seat like if she even lifted one butt cheek, the devil would shoot out from the ground and suck her into the hell where her daughter already had VIP seating.

"When I said church, I meant Christ-centered," she said, finally breaking the thick silence that accompanied us on the car ride home.

"Oh. Okay. Next time," I'd said.

Her Los Angeles memorial was the next time. With Spin Class Chuck, my mom definitely wouldn't have a Christ-centered memorial, but I reasoned it away: If she were looking down at Chuck's spin classes, it looked just like a Baptist church—good music, shouting people, and occasionally someone passed out.

⟋‾‾‾‾⟍

Chuck led fifteen Los Angeles–based people through a living room Mom memorial that was equal parts reverent and celebratory. He said a few sweet words about the love he saw in my mom during his plant-gifting visit and emphasized how everyone gathered had played a part in her peaceful transition. As he neared the memorial finish line, he asked us all to hold hands and share one favorite memory of my mom.

Oh, dear Jesus. No. Wrong question, Chuck!

Mom's memorial was my first ever memorial. I'd been to my grandparents' funerals and there was no question-and-answer portion of the service. I thought that a memorial was what you did when there was no casket for people to view and that it would have the same format as a funeral. I'd given no thought to the fact that the root word of *memorial* is *memories*. This oversight mattered: Like Chuck, most of the memorial guests had no real memories with my mom; they'd met her while she was sound asleep. In addition, most of the memorial attendees were the types of friends who had enough free time to attend a last-minute memorial invite. They were new friends, the types of companions one gathers because they're also out of work and lost half their friends in a divorce. Esteemed guests who could make the midweek invite included a girl who volunteered with me shoveling horse shit and Jim, Byron's handyman friend who installed the grab bars by my mom's toilet. A few guests bought "plus-ones" who'd never even met my mom. In my exhaustion from death chores, I'd put Byron in charge of the guest list, reasoning that a memorial was just pageantry and didn't matter; it's not like it would change that my mother was dead. When Chuck asked everyone for memories, suddenly it mattered a lot. I knew Mom did not want to listen to memories about how cute she looked when she drooled in her sleep, which is the only way most of these folks knew her.

Chuck pointed to Jim the Handyman to start us off.

"Uh. . . . uh . . . my favorite memory . . . was how Byron told me she smiled when she saw there was a grab bar by the toilet," Jim said, sharing a bathroom memory of Mom that would be dismissed in court as hearsay.

I glared at the rest of the guests, their faces displayed various levels of trepidation, much like unprepared schoolkids hoping the teacher doesn't call on them. Chuck nodded to Jim's left. A plus-one—whose name I won't even pretend to remember—admitted she didn't really know my mom well, but from what she'd heard, she was "really really nice." That answer wasn't as bad as it could have been so I loosened my death grip on Byron's hand and also released some of my nervousness, remembering it was a positive that most of my new Los Angeles friends were also out-of-work creatives. Like me, they probably filled their free time with improv classes. If my mom had to die and get eulogized in a strange city, Los Angeles was the best choice; we know how to fake on-the-spot sincerity.

Last up in sharing memories was Melissa, Jim the Handyman's girlfriend. She was also a plus-one. I was rooting for her to wrap up the memorial by reminiscing on a fourth-person account of the deft way my mom slurped down nutrition shakes, or perhaps Melissa would realize how lucky she was to go last—she had clues from other people's memories to help her out.

"I . . . didn't really know her. Pass," Melissa mumbled, then looked down at the living room floor that I'd forced myself to clean prior to everyone's arrival. I gripped the hell out of Byron's hand even though Chuck had instructed us to drop hands and enjoy the fast-food fried chicken Byron had picked up for the post-memorial meal. My grip on Byron's hand was to telepath: *I know this bitch didn't just pass on my mom! Do something!* I fantasized about flying across my living room and snatching the fast food out of Melissa's hand: *If you pass on my mom, you also pass on free chicken!* Instead of joining everyone for fast food, I excused myself and hurried downstairs to my old friend, the toilet seat. I sat on the closed cover, fuming as I texted for Byron to join me.

"I want Jim's girlfriend out," I said once Byron closed the bathroom door.

"What? Why?"

"She passed on my mom! This is a memorial, not a game show!"

"You want me to kick someone out of your mom's memorial?"

"Yes, I don't know her, you do."

"Not really. Jim just started dating her."

"Well, Jim should break up with her! She didn't even bring a card. Why'd you invite someone who wouldn't even bring a card?! Even my old, mean babysitter sent a fucking card," I said.

"Why does a card matter?"

"Are you kidding me, Byron?" I asked, rolling my eyes at how stupid people with alive moms could be. Unlike my brother, Byron seemed to always need a decoder ring for why certain moves post-Mom were important. This was my mom's memorial. Despite her not really knowing a damn person there, I still needed it to go perfectly. I needed to be able to tell everyone in Philadelphia that I was an amazing daughter who had sent her mom off in the proper way.

"I mean, I can kick Melissa out, but do you *really* think that's what your mom would want?" Byron asked, throwing back in my face the phrase I often used to challenge myself. The times when I got the most frustrated were always times when I thought I wasn't living up to "What My Mom Would Want." My mom would want my brother to move in. My mom would want me to not be mad at billboards. My mom wouldn't want people memorializing how she drooled. I knew she definitely would not want me to kick Melissa out; if anything, my mom would have welcomed her twice as warmly for taking the time to attend a stranger's memorial.

"Yes, my mother would want you to kick Melissa out! My mom hated people who don't bring sympathy cards," I lied. I wondered if I sounded insane to Byron. I thought about all the things that seemed sane to me before my mom passed. Like sending "sorry for your loss" flowers. Now I thought it was cruel that people gifted me with something I'd have to watch die. I couldn't teach them all, but their fellow nongrieving normie Melissa was going to learn that day! I flung open the bathroom door, prepared to stomp upstairs and show Melissa how a good memorial eviction was done. As I got one foot on the stairs, I heard Melissa and the other memorial guests burst into cheers. *What the hell?*

Everyone was watching a tennis match, unaware I was behind them. I froze because, damn, watching tennis during a memorial seemed even worse than passing on a turn. Melissa had disrespected my mom, but now everyone was lounging around on the last couch Mom had sat on and cheering for tennis balls. Everyone seemed to be taunting me, showing off that they could pass on moms dying and do normal things like sit on couches without crying and watch sports. I wanted all of them out. I hated them because their actions showed they had no idea how much pain I was in.

I now realize people can't see what you are scared to show. Okay, and I also now realize that new friends made in job fair lines aren't the best people to expect to understand your pain. My overarching point still stands: With most people, besides my brother, I kept insisting, in my mom's favorite words, "I'm fine." I'd try to only cry or get angry in secret, like alone in a bathroom. To absolve myself from covering up my pain like my mom did, I'd reasoned that people know how to help with physical pain like cancer; once my mom took off her scarf, I knew I would do whatever I could to make her lumps disappear. But my pain was internal. That kind of pain, I knew from experience, tends to scare and confuse people. So I hid it. *I'm fine.*

Hanging in there. Yes, I was hanging in there only because the trucks I'd prayed to hit me and end it all never did. That is, when I could even gather the strength to go outside near truck routes.

I stared at the tennis watchers, preparing to practice being more vocal about my pain by kicking them the hell out of my house. I debated which method of kicking them out would be best, a method my mom would approve of like turning off the TV and pointing toward the front door wordlessly; or my way, screaming *I fucking swear I'm telling my mom to tell God to smite all y'all for this disrespectful tennis shit.* I settled on the latter because screaming would probably give my brain some relief, much like an exhausting session in Chuck's spin class. As I took a step toward my guests, my phone rang. Its caller ID flashed one of those names I couldn't ignore, Geraldine, my mom's close work friend.

Geraldine had come to my mom's house to say goodbye and, once my mom was in Los Angeles, called her daily. She'd never seemed suspicious when Mom was too tired to talk, she'd just ask me to put her on speaker and near Mom's ear. I'd listened in as Geraldine told my mom how much she loved and admired her. She'd keep Mom up-to-date about goings-on at the hospital and let her know that absolutely positively no one was mad at her for leaving unfinished work.

Geraldine asked how I was. "I'm fine. Hanging in here," I said. "Just about finished up with my mom's memorial."

"Yep, I heard you were having it in California. I know you made it as beautiful as she was."

"I think I did," I said, while moving my conversation away from my guests, so Geraldine couldn't hear the "beautiful" service being punctuated by tennis cheers.

"Well, don't want to bother you, just wanted you to know we're doing something special for your mom at the hospital," she said, telling me they were having a small memorial on her nursing floor and putting up a plaque after the ceremony. "She'll be the first Black RN to have her own hospital plaque. It's next week if you can make it," she said, mimicking the same words I'd instructed my brother to use when telling Mom's friends that her memorial would be in Los Angeles: "If you can make it" equaled "if you loved her enough."

Of course I had to find a way to make it. Other than my brother, no one loved her as much as me. And I knew he was going to make it, since the lucky bastard lived ten minutes from the hospital. I'd be damned if I contributed to the nurse watercooler talk about how only the sane child attended her memorial. But more than that, Geraldine's call seemed to gently remind me that my mom didn't need to be hoarded anymore. If I was grown enough to give her a good death and realize that she was more than just her body, I had to be grown enough to accept that she was also more than just my mom. She was a trusted friend, a woman in a poetry group, a woman who loved her co-workers and even if I felt they'd gotten too much of her, this plaque was them wanting to do something for her in return. In that moment, I was grateful there were friends like Geraldine feeling even a pinch of the same loss I felt. People who needed an outlet for their grief, people who wouldn't pass on their turn to share memories and, while doing so, perhaps give me another view of the multitudes of my mom. Maybe my anger at how her life had been cut short wouldn't feel so lonely if I shared it. I was all for that as long as I didn't have to plan out any logistical shit like where to buy a plaque. After grief chores, two failed burials at sea, and her Los

Angeles memorial where I tried to convince my boyfriend to kick a girl out, I didn't have any energy left.

I told Geraldine that I would be at my mom's hospital's memorial. I imagined Geraldine's co-workers asking how the call went: *Okay, I think. Though I'm not sure what kind of memorial she was having. In the background, someone shouted "Dammit, ref, are you blind?" Gwen did tell me that her daughter took her to one of those California cult churches.*

After hanging up, my anger at my guests seemed to transform into competitiveness toward my mom's co-workers. I couldn't let her colleagues one-up me by having the only Philly memorial. Besides learning how not to hoard my mom, being an adult also meant mustering up the "twice as hard" energy Mom taught me grown women need to have. Still, my mind was making plans that my body didn't feel strong enough to handle. Instead of being angry no one offered me help, I wondered if it was okay to ask for it. With the room still fixated on tennis, I retreated back down to the toilet and dialed Aunt Jeanette. If she had enough connects to get scones in West Philly back in the '80s, I knew she had enough connects to put together a memorial service.

"I think you may be right. It would be nice to have a memorial in Philly," Aunt Jeanette said, letting me pretend a Philly memorial was my idea.

"I'm not sure where to start," I said, cautiously gearing up to ask for her help. "I mean, mom's fake preacher husband blew through so many churches, she doesn't really have a church home," I said, greasing the conversation's runway with *it ain't entirely my fault I can't do this alone like y'all superwomen would do.*

"We'll have a memorial at your cousin's church," Aunt Jeanette said plainly, putting an abrupt stop to my babbling ask. Her son, my cousin, was not a heathen like me. He was a deacon—which I'm not even really sure what that entails—but I'd gotten my help, so I ended the conversation and emailed her my mom's superlong list of co-workers and friends. I then went back upstairs and watched tennis with the near strangers who had gathered to help me, in the best way they could, memorialize my mom. I wasn't mad at them anymore; in fact, the more I sat, the more I thought my mom might even be pleased with the living room sports celebration. No one was worrying, no one was fussing over her; they were simply being themselves and watching the TV she'd once enjoyed. After the last guest left with a plate of take-home fast food, I turned off my phone to write my mom's obituary, the only death chore my aunt had given me.

13

Mom Wants and Cheap Wine

In the days before the Philly memorial as I tried to write that obituary, I quickly realized that I had no idea how to sum up Mom and *every single thing* she meant to *every single person* while also putting that summary in the right grammatical and emotional order. I couldn't figure out how to make her life—including all the parts I had just recently learned about—into short paragraphs that would fit onto the back of a program. After days of trying, I'd come up with only four sentences. I gave up and texted them to my brother.

> **Me:** How's this read? "Gwen Nissel was born in Philly and raised there. Until she had to move out because of her bum-ass husband. She was surrounded by love as she passed. Because she was with her kids, not her bum-ass husband."
>
> **Jack:** Hahahaha! No notes! Please read that in Philly. I'll read half of it with you!

As much as Mom and I butted heads over my inability to follow her straight and narrow path, I definitely wasn't as gangster as she thought. I knew I couldn't read that obituary. Though I am not her perfect Christ-centered child, there was something scary about possibly offending him in his own home. Plus, even if Christ shared my brother's and my humor, my mom's co-workers probably did not. I imagined the horrified looks on their faces as I read a very undignified obituary about my very dignified mom. I texted my brother again.

Me: Don't kill me. I chickened out. I'm writing a boring obituary.

Jack: I wouldn't kill you, then you'd be chilling with Mom and I'd have to clean out two houses this weekend. Fuck that.

I stopped stressing over the obituary having to be some National Book Award–winning magnum opus. No one would be at the memorial shaking their heads like, *Her grieving daughter's no Audre Lorde, but I guess this will do.* I searched "free sample obituary" and pasted my mom's info into it; when it came to the last sentence—who she was survived by—I wondered if I should include Bill. I knew my mom would want him included and she'd fear people's judgment if they found out she wasn't the happy preacher's wife she'd pretended to be. I wanted the opposite of what she'd have wanted. I wanted people to know she was brave and had left a bad situation instead of dying in it. I met in the middle of my mom's wants and my own; I put Bill's name last and left out his "Reverend" title. It was just a hint of shade when I felt I was entitled to high levels of sass, but still, I debated if I was embarrassing my mom in death. If I embarrassed her at her own memorial, I wasn't sure I could forgive myself. I sent my brother the completed obituary and asked for his feedback on putting Bill's name last.

Jack: If anyone says shit to you about name placement in Mom's memorial program, I will drive my fucking minivan through the stained-glass windows. Promise.

As the pilot announced we were making our descent into Philadelphia, I tried to do what I always did when flying home; I looked down at the city searching for the first place I recognized. Not well-known places like stadiums, but the small parks and streets among the row houses, places that had personal meaning to my mom and me. I noticed Fairmount Park, where Mom taught me how to roller-skate. She'd almost fallen into the Delaware River because wet park grass is not a safe place to wear tiny wheels on your feet. Usually her surviving a near fall into a polluted river would be a happy memory, but a sudden heaviness came over me. *This city is no longer home if there's no Mom to see.* I realized that I'd taken for granted that we'd have more time to create memories. I stopped looking out of the window.

While I was grateful my aunt and cousin had arranged the memorial, and I numbly forced on a smile as I thanked people for coming, it was overwhelming seeing how much of my mom's life I still knew nothing about. I'd made that big, deep claim about wanting to see her multitudes, but every person who was a stranger felt like evidence of my own shortcomings. *I should have spent more time with her. I should know these people. Why didn't we talk more after she married Bill?*

The church was packed to capacity by the time I took my front-row seat. I turned around to take in the guests, scanning each row, curious if Bill had dared to show up. I imagined him dramatically entering and releasing his funeral pigeons, which made me laugh out loud, then I felt self-conscious for laughing because that's not what you do when your mom is dead. I wondered if people were judging me for not crying. I judged myself for not crying, but it's hard to cry when you're numb. That's all I remember feeling. Numb. Like I put on a coat of armor to travel back to Philadelphia and trudge through the long list of things you're supposed to do when your mom dies and I hoped everyone thought I did a good job. I do remember no one in the crowd asked me where Reverend Bill was. I guessed the watercooler talk my mom had feared judging her for taking a "vacation" had already covered the topic of her marriage. I also remember my aunt's minister telling me that I had to carry the torch of my mom's life. I couldn't think of carrying a whole-ass torch of a life when I barely had the strength to carry myself back to one city. I remember feeling relieved when the memorial was over only to learn that it was not.

"You have to receive people," Aunt Jeanette explained as I beelined straight for the memorial cake after the preacher's last "amen." My aunt redirected me from hiding near the cake and placed me near the church's entrance, where people had formed a line that snaked through several pews. Like the service, I don't remember much of what people said. I remember wanting badly to be a smart-ass whenever someone would tell me my mom was in a better place. *My house is actually very nice* I wanted to reply. I didn't. I knew they meant well. I simply smiled my way through the condolences that all seemed to blur together.

Except for two people's condolences.

A co-worker of my mom's whose name I can't remember told me that Mom often bragged about me and that I'd turned out so well.

I thanked her for her kind words like I'd thanked the dozens of co-workers and friends before her. Instead of hugging me and moving toward the cake, she continued.

"I remember you were pretty touch-and-go for a while," she said then leaned in closer like she was going to share a secret. "I remember her going to see you in the psych ward. Please know she loved you so much even though she was probably very embarrassed."

I wanted to say, *Bitch, I was embarrassed too! You think I wanted to be crazy?* But I didn't because, again, I'm not as gangster as my mom thought. Even now, as I think back to her coworker's words, I feel self-conscious that the woman may read this and feel badly. We all say awkward things at really bad times. Maybe not *bringing up someone's psych diagnosis while they're barely holding it together through their mom's memorial in a town that no longer feels like home* bad, but thanks to her, I had more appreciation for the people who stuck to the standard, yet hurtful, "Your mom is in a better place."

The second person whose receiving line exchange I clearly remember had also dared to venture away from meaningless grief chatter. He arrived alone and as I saw him lingering after most of the crowd had departed, I second-guessed churches having an open-door policy and assumed Bill had hired a hit man to take me out until the lone man also gushed about how proud my mom was.

"She was always talking about you. How you are a big Hollywood producer," he said, then asked if I minded waiting while he fetched his book of poems. He was a member of my mom's poetry group.

"I don't mean to impose, but I think it really has potential," he said, his tone more gleeful than anyone else in the receiving line. I desperately wanted to burst his bubble and tell him there was no one in Hollywood hoping I'd come back with poems, that no one in Hollywood even cared if I came back at all, that my dead mom's coming disability check was the only reason I could even pay my bills for the next few months.

"Sure! I know some actors who love poems," I lied, because that's what my mom would want, people talking about how generous her successful daughter was.

She's not like those other Hollywood folks. She's real. That's what the nurses would now say around their watercooler.

After I had taken possession of the thick stack of poems, my brother whispered, "This is bullshit. I'll be in the car."

"Keep it running," I replied.

———

After escaping the church, I rode shotgun and glanced back at my nephew, wondering if he knew why the hell his father and I were suddenly going to church. He was lost in his tablet. I was amazed at how unaffected he was. His young brain didn't seem to understand grief. I wondered if it was because he was so young and he had only recently emerged from the same afterlife his grandmom was now in.

"Do you think Mom is where Jay was before he was born? Like, where are people before they were born?" I asked my brother.

"I think your edible finally kicked in," he replied.

He was right. He'd offered me one to take the edge off the memorial. I laughed and kept my existential questions to myself, grateful that it was just my brother and me. We could finally take off the fake, numb smiles. We could relax and be ignorant without embarrassing our mom.

We were gearing up to do yet another death chore: cleaning our mom's home from top to bottom to prepare it for probate sale. The probate lawyer handling Mom's estate had mentioned he knew a Realtor who could clear it out for us, freeing us from what he'd described as "the trouble" of doing so ourselves. I'd decided that the real estate agent was trouble himself, a colonizer intent on stealing all the history in Mom's house. I knew the agent would stick a sign on my mom's front lawn announcing an estate sale and I also knew from being a customer at many of those while looking for LL Cool J T-shirts that she would not want strangers digging through her bedroom drawers. After absolutely hating our other death chores, I'd convinced my brother that cleaning out Mom's house would be different. It wouldn't involve waiting on hold, or even customer service. It would be only the two of us, our favorite pairing.

"It'll be fun," I'd said. I'd told him it would be like one last Christmas together. That being surrounded by so many of Mom's things would make us spiritually closer to her. That her energy was still in her clothes and we had to be the ones to harness it, not strangers looking for a good eBay flip. We'd protect her energy by keeping a few items, then find a women's health charity to donate the rest to. That's what our mom would want us to do.

After less than five minutes of cleaning, the edible was not enough and I left to buy wine. Mom's closets were stuffed. She shopped a lot. She was one of those middle-aged ladies who pre-bought Christmas gifts, then bought more in case she accidentally forgot someone. She'd buy things at thrift stores just because "someone might be able to use it." When the fall arrived in Philadelphia, she'd send me a care package of summer clothes she bought on sale with notes saying "Love you! I know you can always use short sleeves in California!" I never thought about how she stored her generous and sale-loving nature in a small row house. I realized that cleaning out just one stuffed closet would be hours of manual labor, labor I'd have to do through tears. The closet reminded me that I'd never get another summer sale care package. That I'd never visit another thrift store with her. Why on earth had I thought that touching her things would be healing? It hurt worse than looking down at landmarks from twenty thousand feet above. I didn't want to give up because I'd convinced my brother it would be fun, so I just drank more wine until he came upstairs and found me surrounded by empty moving boxes and Mom's closet completely untouched.

"Fuck this," I sniffled out to my brother, glad for one person who wouldn't judge me for being too drunk to safely carry our mother's torch or clean out her home. I grabbed one bad-ass 1970s sweater from her closet and told my brother that I was going to sleep.

"I don't want to do this shit either," my brother said and stopped pretending he was really going to harness Mom's energy by cleaning under her bathroom sink. "This was a horrible idea," he said, laughing.

I admitted it was. "How come nobody at the memorial offered to help us with this?" I asked, like I had ever myself offered to help anyone clean out a house.

"Because everybody sucks," my brother said.

I agreed. If sucking meant that no one else on earth felt the pain that we felt sitting surrounded by the smells and textures that made up our mom's life, then everyone except my brother and I positively sucked.

My brother found a for-profit thrift store that did last-minute pickups. My mother would still have people going through her drawers, and none of her things would go to charity. I got mad at myself because that's not what she would have wanted. That seemed to be my cycle. I'd stopped being mad at billboards because that's not what she would have wanted and instead got mad at myself for not being a better daughter. A better daughter would be able to effortlessly clean out her mom's house then hand out her many coats to the homeless. Instead, I thumbed through Mom's coats to make sure I wasn't leaving a "good" one behind for the thrift store to pick up.

"Why would someone donate a coat this nice to a thrift store?" my brother mimed in our mother's voice as he saw the faux fur I was taking for myself. That was one of her rituals, showing off her thrift store finds while wondering aloud why in the heck someone would donate a designer coat to Goodwill.

"Because someone died, Mom," I said.

My brother and I laughed.

"She wouldn't want us to clean this mess," he said. "She'd say we were fussing over her." I nodded even though I knew my brother was simply trying to make me feel better that my plans to bond over moving boxes had dissolved into us on the floor together drinking cheap wine.

"You know what I do think Mom would want?" I asked. "You gotta promise not to laugh."

"I won't laugh."

"For me to become a nurse like her."

"Why would I laugh at that? That's perfect," my brother said. He listened as I told him the research I'd done and how many credits would transfer from my BA. Looking up nursing schools was the only thing I found pleasure in doing. I told him my plans of starting as soon as he and his family moved in the new year.

"I've already been looking for elementary schools for Jay," he said. "You know that's what Mom would want—gotta get that education."

"Yep, you know Mom. She thought that fixed everything," I said. We often joked that if one of us came home stabbed or shot, our mom would say it wouldn't have happened if we'd gotten master's degrees.

Instead of packing up Mom's things, we sat on her floor and made more Los Angeles plans. My brother would get his California electrical license and start his own business. His wife, who was also looking forward to the move, would start a catering company. With all three of us working and living together, we didn't have to barely make ends meet while hoping we had enough left over to afford plane tickets to see each other on Christmas. We'd be taking care of each other, like we'd promised Mom.

"I love you so fucking much," I said. Before Mom passed, I can't remember if I'd ever stopped in the middle of a conversation to tell my brother that I loved him. That I loved him was always a given, but now that he was all I had, I found it important for him to know as much as possible. His willingness to start a new Los Angeles life like Mom did gave me something to hold on to. I congratulated us on making it through all the biggest death chores besides Bill's lawsuit as we swigged wine straight out of the bottle and fell asleep on her bedroom floor.

14

Church Organs and Cheap Men

I became addicted to refreshing my email and getting the latest updates on Bill's lawsuit. I happily imagined how angry Bill was that I was fighting his every claim and not staying quiet and respectable like my mom. Perhaps in retaliation for how hard I was fighting him, Bill had added an addendum to his original lawsuit of wedding rings and buffalo nickels. He also wanted dried flowers, a church organ, and an extension cord.

I wondered if I was the only person in the history of the world who had been sued for an extension cord.

Bill added another addendum to his addendums and claimed he was supposed to receive my mom's disability check and that I'd changed the beneficiary without her permission.

"That dickhead ain't even ask for his birds?" my brother asked, incredulous. My brother was the new full-time caretaker of the holy pigeon flock. While he ranted about how much birds cost to feed, I was obsessed with being sued for an extension cord. I was determined to channel the anger I felt toward myself into making Bill's life a legal living hell.

———

". . . and a fucking extension! He's suing me for an extension cord!" I yelled out to Byron. He'd asked why I always seemed to be typing lawyer emails since arriving back from Philly. Byron tried often to nudge me to do anything besides constantly emailing lawyers, scanning wedding ring receipts, and Google-searching other people's experiences with being sued by their stepdads. There were more search results for that than there were for hospice reviews.

"Want to take a break and grab lunch?" Byron asked.

"No! I don't want to eat lunch. I don't need lunch. My mom will never have another lunch again! You don't understand; Bill is not going to treat me like he treated my mom!" I paused to find the stupidest item Bill was claiming my brother and I had stolen. "Christmas tree lights! He's suing me over my dead mom's fucking Christmas tree lights! If you don't understand how much my mom loved Christmas and her little Black Santas and why I have to avenge her and her Christmas tree lights, then I don't know what to tell you, Byron!"

And that's enough for a boyfriend to nod his head and say, "Okay, no lunch. I'll leave you to your legal email."

I responded to Bill's latest addendum.

Dear two lawyers:

I hope this finds you well. I must admit that I find myself

decidedly not well. I'm mortified at what a petty man my mom married. If she weren't already dead, she would surely keel over in embarrassment reading that he's suing me for dried flowers and an extension cord. Here is my official response:

1. Wedding ring set. I have them. I also attached the receipts for them because Bill was unemployed and my mom purchased her own wedding ring set. She also bought his wedding band. Should I countersue him for that shit? I will. Let me know.

2. Organ. That out-of-tune church relic is currently sitting on a dusty for-profit thrift shop sales floor. My brother and I had to lie to the donation hotline and say we had "generic musical equipment" for pickup because no one wanted that damn organ, not even for free. Apparently, gas is worth more than that shit. Please note, there was also a mouse in it.

3. Extension cord? What kind of bus stop lawyer even takes a case with a grown-ass man suing a daughter for extension cords? Seriously, he can fuck off with that.

Thank you both for reading.

This was just a small slice of the email; the final numbered list was just shy of four pages. If I were to print out every email I sent my lawyers, I can guarantee it would at least be novella-length. In contrast, here are the longest emails I sent my divorce lawyer:

He wants what? Will call.
No. Will call.
TY. Yes. Will call!!

Short and to the point. No salutations at the top and no perfectly formatted lists. I'd overthink using exclamation points as I didn't know how many punctuation marks my husband was using in his legal emails and by law, I had to pay for both of our divorce lawyers. Defending my mom's insolvent estate, however, I became verbose because winning against Bill was the last chance I had to do right by her. She had only asked me to save her house, but I knew that I would also spend every disability dollar fighting for her extension cords because it was what she deserved. I also wanted Bill to know that *I* knew that she deserved so much better than him.

During the weeks Mom lived with me, there was one conversation we'd had that continually fueled my fight against Bill. When she and I weren't arguing over dinner orders or butt-wiping and were dipping our toes into some of those real, emotional adult talks I wanted, she had started chatting about her marriage. Her perspective on Bill had shifted; she was done feeling stupid and was instead asking why she chose to put up with a marriage where she was unhappy.

"I mean, he couldn't find joy in nothing," Mom had said. "At one point, I thought maybe I wasn't dying fast enough for him," she'd continued, a tinge of amusement in her voice.

I was not amused. That sentence was not even a little bit of a joke to me; it became my motivation, my personal Bat Signal. Whenever I thought of devoting less energy to constantly refreshing my email and avenging my mom's honor, I'd put that sentence on repeat in my head and think, *Oh really? That's all the energy you got to fight against someone who made your mom feel she wasn't dying quickly enough? What kind of daughter are you?!* I'd berate myself and remind myself of how hard she fought cancer. *Your mom survived multiple rounds of chemo and radiation and you're complaining that your eyes hurt from staring at a screen? Why are you so weak? Harriet Tubman would have shot you.*

I would have done anything for five more minutes with my mom and there was someone still alive who made her feel like she had died too slowly. When friends called, I hurried them off the phone because I had to do research on fair market values of buffalo nickels and church organs. Since my mom's disability money wasn't enough to actually hire a competent sniper and flee to a nonextradition country, I continued researching and banging out those long lawyer emails without concern for the price tag. There was no getting Mom back, but I could get back at the person who'd had her and didn't appreciate it. Three weeks after she passed, I still had no job, but I worked a daily shift making sure Non-Reverend Bill knew I was staying up his ass like the hemorrhoids he couldn't get fixed until he met my mom and her good health insurance.

Just like I had grand plans for how much of a bonding experience cleaning out Mom's home would be, I became the quarterback to what I saw as the familial team sport of battling a sixty-seven-year-old man. I cc'ed my brother on every email. I put him in charge of getting statements from Mom's neighbors. I flew back to

Philadelphia to testify in his criminal trial against Bill and paid for plane wi-fi solely to research if a sixty-seven-year-old could do hard time for threatening someone with a hammer. Once I disembarked the flight, I thought about scooting by the TSA desk. I wished I had some of my mom's ashes, so I could show that supervisor how horrible he was not to give me her cane.

You said she can get her cane when she gets back! Well, dammit, she's back! I'd say and leave the ashes on his desk. Because of his own policies, he'd have to keep her ashes there forever because the owner was never ever coming back to claim them.

Once at my brother's house, after everyone was asleep, I reviewed court cases into the night just like I'd studied the BCB. I studied strategies for juries, learned how much Bill's intent mattered in sentencing, and forwarded compelling cases to my brother, arguing he needed to at least skim them by the morning so our district attorney would know that we knew our gotdamn rights.

At Family Court, my brother, his son, and I were placed in the kids' waiting room. It didn't seem to have been updated since my mom and I spent time there in the eighties. While Mom was probably embarrassed that she had to take her eight-year-old daughter to the courthouse, I loved Family Court days. They were days I got to be alone—for hours—with her. Because I was a child, I had no idea that sitting for hours in a room built for children is not fun for adults and that we were only there so long because custody and support courts are excruciatingly slow. To me, the children's waiting room was the happy room where my mom practiced math with me. It was the room where she taught me how to spell grown-up words like *continuance*.

As an adult stepping into that same room, I realized she had only taught me how to spell *continuance* because she was trying to protect me. Just like she'd done with her finances and soda cans, she was trying to protect me from grown folks' problems by hiding them beneath an educational lesson. Instead of that sudden realization making me grateful for her, it added more fuel to my Bill fire; I saw defeating Bill as delayed justice against years of courthouse failure.

"We're sending that piece of shit Bill to jail," I said to my brother, carefully keeping my cursing hushed from the nearby kids on laps. I needed to know that my brother was still on the same team as I, the team intent on sending another body to the criminal industrial complex we were both extremely against. Except, of course, when it came to Bill.

In response to my rallying cry, my brother nodded in agreement. He quietly nodded at most of my court coaching. I didn't care if he was nonverbal, as long as he heard me. I saw myself as an understanding sister; I knew that he, as a parent, couldn't devote as much effort as I could to avenging our mom. I researched more statutes while he teed up another alphabet video for his son.

After about an hour of waiting, Christine, our district attorney, entered. She was clearly overworked and immune to the chaos of the kids' waiting room. Though she was wearing high heels, she deftly stepped over playing toddlers before reading to us from a very unorganized manila file folder. I remember clearly seeing the name of another defendant on one of her file papers. I also remember looking away thinking, *I'm not supposed to see that*, then thinking, *What would I even do with that information? Find their number, call them up and say, "When I was in the kids' court waiting room I saw your name. Hahaha! You have a fucked-up family life too!"*

Christine went over a few courtroom rules, then something in our file caught her eye. "Do you know a Clarence Tucker?" she asked us. My brother and I replied that we did not.

"Clarence is apparently Bill's character witness," she said. "I'm pretty sure he hired Clarence from the fountain outside." The fountain she was referring to was an aboveground pool-size water sculpture directly across from the courthouse. The sculpture's original purpose was to honor the Native Americans who owned the land, now it was mostly used by folks who barely owned anything to take a daily bath.

"Bill would definitely hire a guy from the fountain," I said. "That's why he needs jail time," I added, making sure Christine knew she was joining a team with a ready-made plan. I had decided we'd settle for nothing less than six months in jail.

"Does he think I don't know all the homeless guys who bathe across the street? I work here," Christine continued, blowing past my jail time comment. She then sighed like she'd thought she'd seen it all, but a defendant hiring a character witness he'd met in a fountain was some new shit she could entertain her family with over dinner.

"Can we hire our own district attorney?" I asked my brother after Christine rushed off to deal with her overloaded schedule. I knew there must be some secret district attorney rich people use.

A private-practice DA who wasn't underpaid and overworked. "We need someone focused," I said, reasoning that if we used the same burnt-out government attorneys our mom had used in child support court, we'd get the same results she had—not a damn thing.

"Let's both look up rich people district attorneys," I said. I wanted Bill to know he messed with the wrong family, for him to eventually get shanked over ramen noodles and such victory would only be possible with a private practice DA. As my brother opened his phone's browser to start what would be a fruitless "rich people district attorney" search, I thought of other tasks that could ensure we would get the results Mom deserved.

"Do you think Jay'll cry?" I asked my brother.

"Naw, he'll be fine. Jay won't cry,"

"No, we need him to cry," I insisted. "Doesn't he know his father could have died?"

"No, he literally only remembers the indoor water fight."

Seriously? Mom's protective lessons got him too? Great, now I'm going to cry, I thought.

"Either you or my nephew has to cry. We have to stand out from these other families," I said, throwing out more strategies to get a judge or jury on our side. I reminded him of the court tips I'd read online: "Don't be afraid to make eye contact, speak slowly, try not to stutter—"

"Sis, calm down, no one is sending an old man who claims to be a reverend to jail."

"Well, maybe they would if you'd have just let him hit you a little bit," I countered. "I mean, of course, not enough to get *really* hurt or anything," I added before telling my brother that his deft reflexes were the reason Bill was fighting the lesser charge of attempted assault instead of aggravated. I was victim-blaming my brother for not being more of a victim.

"I'm hungry," my nephew, Jay, said, returning to the safety of our side after learning it's hard to retrieve a tablet once you've offered it to other bored kids.

"Well, let's hunt and see what we can find," my brother replied, his tone reminding me that gentle dad mode was his normal mode. I could also tell this quick dip out to find food was because I was annoying the hell out of him.

Once inside the courtroom, I was separated from my brother and he was probably grateful. As Christine ushered my brother and nephew to a spot reserved for plaintiffs, Bill entered with his attorney, an exhausted-looking younger man in a suit at least one size too big. I stared at Bill. He caught my eye and then looked away.

I tried not to laugh out loud as Bill's attorney seemed confused as to whether he was even representing Bill. As he and Bill embarrassingly went back and forth about a bounced check, I knew from my court research that everything a judge sees can unconsciously influence how he rules. Without my brother and I saying one word, Bill was proving he wasn't someone who should be roaming the city streets, he was an arguing check bouncer whose only friend was one he'd borrowed from the fountain. Despite all my court research, I hadn't bothered to learn that witnesses aren't allowed to hear other witness testimony and was surprised to be kicked out into the hallway. Before exiting I gave my brother a look: *Don't fumble our chance to take Bill down.*

After an hour in the hallway, no one had called me in.

"That means his attorney doesn't want you in there," one of the arresting officers said to me, as the first hour stretched into the second.

"Are you serious?"

"Yeah, you're not getting called in this late."

"What about you?" I asked, certain that uniformed officers' account of the night would balance out my nephew's giddy testimony about our familial indoor water fight.

"We get paid overtime even if they don't call us in." The officer shrugged and went back to his phone.

———

"I want another pretzel," Jay said. He and my brother were done testifying. The entire trial was done.

"You don't need me?" I asked Christine.

"Nope, you're good," she said.

"But I flew across the country—"

"Yeah, thank you. We used that to avoid a continuance," she said, then scurried off to use the bathroom before the judge called us all in to issue his ruling. Bill's charge had been argued down from attempted assault to possession of an instrument of crime. The judge sentenced him to twelve months' probation.

"That's not enough," I whispered to Christine, but my whisper was overtaken by Bill's shouting.

"I object!" Bill yelled, staring straight at the judge. "If holding a hammer means I'm guilty of possessing an instrument of crime, then every handyman in this building is also guilty!"

Bill was dead-ass serious.

As his lawyer tugged on Bill's suit sleeve trying to get him to shut up, I thought, *Damn, what my mom really wanted was to get away from this sad little man.* And then I realized that for three weeks of her life, she had done that. When she was having those candid conversations with me about the stupidity of staying in a bad marriage, I wished I had told her how proud I was of her for finally walking away. How amazing it was to be in fear of judgment—God's and everyone else's—and still decide that the most important thing is your own peace.

If I chose to give up against Bill's extension cord and organ claims, I had nothing to fear but my own judgment that somehow my fight to avenge my mom must be directly proportional to how much I loved her. It didn't have to be. She didn't leave my brother and me that disability money for vengeance. She would never overpay for something God handed out for free.

Back in LA, I wrote the shortest email of all:

Dear two lawyers,
What does Bill want to settle?

The reply came quickly. He wanted $5,000.
Five thousand dollars? That wasn't even the retainer for my

lawyers. With my nouveau riche disability-insurance-money-having ass, I forgot how cheap it could be to pay broke dudes to leave you alone. Old broke ones, apparently, were even cheaper.

Of course, because this was Bill, when I refreshed my email, another one popped right up.

> Forget the $5,000. He amended it to $7,500. He forgot he had
> to pay his lawyer 33%.

I wanted badly to be petty and hold firm at five thousand, but more than pettiness and vengeance, I wanted the same peace my mom had when she finally left him. With a few clicks on the computer, I sent my lawyers the money and told my brother that we were finally free of Bill.

15

Jacob, Esau, and Reddit

Of course, once I couldn't fixate on court cases, I had to find something else to fill my time. When my mind was idle, I often cried for no reason, so to keep the tears away, I took over the logistics of my brother's move. I hired moving trucks, personally visited public schools, and had Handyman Jim put up a wall so Jack and his wife could have more privacy. I was certain, of course, that helping rush my brother into my house would make grief easier to get through. I *needed* my brother around. If I was going to continually burst into tears for no reason, I needed someone else around who understood and did the same.

However, in our recent talks, my brother hadn't seemed as eager to move, hinting that, perhaps, there were better things to do with Mom's disability money.

"I could stop renting and buy my own family a house," he'd said.

"Yeah—a really shitty Philly hood fixer-upper," I said, as if the judgy tone of my voice would make my brother forget we grew up very unafraid of "hoods," plus he had an electrician's license, which helps a lot in fixing up shitty homes.

My brother definitely wasn't focused on all the in-person public school research I'd done. I'd even formatted it into a handy spreadsheet, which he admitted he had yet to read. I begged him to read it; application deadlines were approaching. When he finally looked it over, he called me back. He was pissed.

"What's this column you added to the spreadsheet? Must send grades?" my brother asked, jolting me out of my sleep. He kept screaming about how insulting one column on my spreadsheet was. My brother and I had never screamed at each other as adults.

"Why are these schools asking for my son's grades?!"

Wiping sleep from my eyes, I tried to explain that, in my admittedly zero-years' experience being a parent, a school asking for a child's grades didn't seem offensive, but the more I explained, the more he yelled.

"You sure they ask that of everybody?"

"They said it's standard—"

"No, it's not. They think because my son is coming from a Philly public school that he's too dumb for their school," he said before declaring me and the entire Los Angeles school system elitist. "So yeah, fuck this school requirement shit, we're not moving," my brother finally spat out.

"Are you fucking serious? I already paid for a contractor to fix up the bedroom for you and I'm the one who did all this research on the schools—"

My brother interrupted me. "Nobody asked you to do that."

He was very right. I took over everything with the excuse that I had free time and he had a family to attend to, but I took over everything so *I* could also have a family to attend to—his family! He'd just taken that from me.

"Fuck you," I said.

"Fuck you too!"

And in less words than it took to get rid of Bill, my brother was gone. The next day I tried to call him and an automated woman's voice told me his number was no longer in service. He'd blocked me.

What a piece of shit, I thought. He had abandoned me over a spreadsheet. I didn't stop to think that his sudden anger meant he was going through his own grief. Or, for him, maybe blaming schools and spreadsheets was safer than bluntly letting his sister know that moving cross-country to start a mom memorial commune may not be the right choice for his family, or any healthy family, really. In hindsight, it was a horrible idea. At no time in my entire life did I have a dream to share a bathroom with my brother, his wife, and their growing son, but with my mom gone, I was convinced the meaning of life was sharing toilet paper with family.

Jack replaced the billboard blonde as the most-hated person in my life. Then, hating my brother became too much of a burden, so I simply decided he didn't exist. I decided that I didn't need new memories with him, he wasn't the only family I had: I could make a chosen family. I had Byron to create memories with and I'd been pushing him away every chance I got. My last meaningful interaction with Byron was me absolutely losing my shit on him because he had thrown out expired orange juice.

"What the fuck? Why would you throw out the last thing my mom touched?"

Byron tried to explain that it had grown a layer of mold.

"You don't get it," I said, explaining that I didn't care if the bottle had sprouted an orange tree whose branches busted through the refrigerator. I was keeping that orange juice.

"If your mom had died, I wouldn't throw away anything she touched without asking you," I said while thinking, *Damn, how could he not know this?*

I would make up for the orange juice fight with Byron. I would start going out with him and making new brotherless memories.

My first attempt at this self-challenge was being Byron's plus-one at Melissa and Handyman Jim's wedding. At the ceremony, I cooed and clapped with the other guests right up until the reception when the band cued up the couple's first dance song. It was "Somewhere Over the Rainbow."

"That's Gretchen's song. The white acoustic guitar girl," I whispered to Byron, and as some guests dabbed at happy tears over their troubles melting like lemon drops, I wailed the loud scary cry that usually only came out at home. With all eyes suddenly on me and not the bride and groom, I ran out of the venue and called a ride to take me home, leaving Byron alone to explain why his girlfriend had been triggered by a *Wizard of Oz* song. I have no idea how he explained to a just-married couple that their first dance song was also my mother's death song without completely ruining the wedding. I did know if my mom's spirit was looking over me like everyone said it was, she was embarrassed as hell that I was ruining other people's special moments.

Anything that reminded me of Mom or Jack became a trigger to cry. To avoid tears, I had the contractor break down the wall he'd just built. I got human interaction mostly from online grief groups.

For a bit, reading messages from other people in grief was the only thing that made me feel normal. I found community in chatting with other people about how hard it was to get out of bed once a loved one had died. But, soon, even that practice made me feel more alone as grieving people started sharing the signs they'd received from dead loved ones. Those were always the posts with the most engagement.

"A feather appeared on my front step! And I know it's my mom!"

Gushing responses would follow:

"Yes, that feather is your mom!"

"Beautiful, she's telling you she loves you!"

"When feathers appear, angels are near!"

As I read about people whose grief seemed to vanish after seeing one flickering streetlight, I developed anxiety over why my mom hadn't yet sent me a clear afterlife sign. Forget a flickering light—my house was old, that was normal. I asked my mom to knock the Maya Angelou anthology off my shelf and open it to "Phenomenal Woman." That did not happen so I settled for Mom coming to me in a dream. After several dream-free nights, I couldn't even log on to my grief group because I'd break down if I saw another daughter had received a sign and I still hadn't.

I went back to shoveling shit at the rescue barn. After a few days, I found lonely poop duty to be exactly what I needed. You truly have to stay in the moment around horses or you'll get kicked in the head. For hours, I'd simply repeat, "Look for poop, shovel it, don't get kicked in the head" over and over. It was zen. I didn't have to worry about wedding songs making me burst into tears or reading that yet another daughter had seen a heavenly feather.

Then came Elyse.

Elyse was college-aged, a bit awkward in a way I usually find endearing but not when I've lost both my mom and my brother and just want to be alone with horse shit. Elyse was palpably desperate for connection and I wanted nothing more than to avoid connecting. I used my usual tactics of talking about death to make things uncomfortable and shut down conversations. Elyse would make small talk about how pretty the fall leaves were and I'd tell her leaves change colors because they were dying.

"They're dead, Elyse. The tree literally kills its own leaves so it can survive the winter."

Elyse didn't think that was morbid. She'd ask how I was, and I'd reply, "Shitty, my mom just died," and that didn't make Elyse back off like it did most others. Suddenly, every day I was there, Elyse was also there, trying to chat me up.

"Sorry, I was late. I was stuck on the phone making Thanksgiving plans," she said, trying to bait me into more small talk. I did not care if she was late. I wasn't the boss.

"My mom is so anal about the holidays," she continued before suddenly covering her mouth. Her eyes went wide as she realized she'd said the word *mom*. That was nothing new. Since my mom had died, even the rare person like Elyse who could stand morbid jokes tended to apologize for saying the *m*-word around me. I hated that. That people could think I was strong enough to lose an actual mom but weak enough to be taken down by a word felt like misplaced pity. I told Elyse that she could say the word *mom*, that I liked the word *mom* a lot better than the word *brother*.

"Do you have someplace to go for the holidays?" Elyse asked. "My mom wouldn't mind an extra guest."

My only holiday plans were to be completely alone in the house where my mom died. That actually sounded way better than joining Elyse's family. I understood rationally why Elyse—and some of my friends—thought hosting me was a kind gesture, but I hated it. I saw it as offensive.

What did people expect I would get out of spending one of the most important family days of the year around their alive families? *Yes, Elyse. I'd love to come watch you and your very alive mom "not mind" me being there. I look forward to watching you and your mom sharing a Tofurky Roast that my dead mom will never get to taste. If she were alive, she would have tasted it to be polite even though she would have asked me what the hell that thing was on the car ride home. Oh, also, does your mom make everyone go around the table and say what they're grateful for? I hope so! That will be especially fun as I make some shit up before asking where your bathroom is so I can cry alone.*

I lied and told Elyse I had plans.

One day soon after, Elyse asked if I ever noticed proof my mom's spirit was still around. Just like on my message boards, she seemed enamored with signs from beyond the grave.

No, Elyse, she just died and I said, well, that's that! Can't believe I never tried looking for signs from her. What a good idea, I'll pass that along to the other grievers!

"Elyse. I literally shovel shit in a barn that also houses chickens and my mom hasn't sent me one feather," I said.

"Oh, wow," she replied. "Well, I know it's not everyone's thing, but if you ever want someone to help you contact her, let me know. I know a great medium."

And suddenly, Elyse was my new best friend. I stayed past my shift's end to escort Elyse to her locker so she could retrieve her cell phone and hand over that medium's number. Elyse offering her medium was like a billionaire offering my mom his personal oncologist. Unlike me, Elyse wasn't shoveling shit to take her mind off being unemployed as Elyse's rich parents paid for her mucking boots and bills as long as she volunteered somewhere ten hours a week.

"They just believe the world needs more charity and less capitalism," she'd explained and I didn't ask how her parents made their money. That didn't matter. What mattered was they were the rich Los Angelenos I strove to be and as such, I knew they had parties where bestselling spiritual gurus mingled with celebrities and CEOs.

When I was part of the Hollywood in crowd, I'd personally watched a celebrity psychic channel someone's dead dog as a fiftieth birthday gift. The whole party got emotional as the psychic translated barks from heaven. I hadn't believed in psychics until that moment; I grew up on Leviticus and news stories about Miss Cleo bankrupting people. At that party, I learned the Los Angeles elites had their on-call "psychic practitioners" and usually guarded them as tightly as they guarded their mansions. But not Elyse, my new bestie. With the Beverly Hills phone number she handed over, I knew I'd soon have my own story to share on the grief group site. I could finally talk to my mom, the only person I wanted to be around.

16

Short Psychic Break

Despite being done with hope, a little bit rose in my chest before I texted the medium named Claire. I'd researched her online and found her celeb-studded website. Several character actors raved about Claire's abilities, next to their headshots they used words like *gifted* and *brilliant*. Her hourly rate was more than I've paid for used cars yet she had a long waiting list for appointments. Luckily, thanks to Elyse I was one of the chosen ones and had Claire's direct number. When I texted to set our appointment, I used purposefully stilted language, careful not to give Claire any context clues to my personality. All Claire knew was that I wanted to contact my mom and that her first name was Gwen.

As I counted down the days to our call, instead of avoiding my online grief group, I jumped back into it, soaking up others' after-life experiences to prepare for my own. Someone dropped a tip that spirits like clean spaces so I buffed my home to a shine it hadn't seen since it was built during World War II. I cleaned tiles with a toothbrush, I learned how to bleach grout. No mildew was going to come between me and Mom.

Everything about Claire's phone personality let me know I was in good hands. Her slightly raspy voice made her sound folksy, like a New Age aunt who couldn't quit her Marlboro habit. She started the call all business; she knew I was paying for a ride to the afterlife and her job was to get me there within an hour. Her confidence made me suddenly anxious. I had a feeling Claire wouldn't flinch before telling me bad news. I pictured her telling me she couldn't reach Mom because she'd died yet again, this time out of disappointment at me and my brother.

"I promise you," Claire said. "You're going to talk to her. I've been doing this a long time. Your mom's consciousness is not gone, only her physical body."

"If her consciousness answers you, please ask it why it has been ignoring me for months," I said.

Claire took a pregnant pause as if listening to something. I worried my mom was wasting precious time by apologizing: *I'm so sorry my daughter bothered you and your lovely psychic gift. It's been the stress of my cancer.* Instead, Claire exhaled a long, frustrated breath.

"Your mom hasn't been ignoring you. She's tried to talk to you. Many times."

"What? When?" I asked, trying to think back on any signs I'd missed.

"She said you didn't notice because you've got a hard head," Claire said, then sighed.

Did Claire just tell me I was hardheaded, then sigh? She was *definitely* channeling my mom. I laughed in disbelief. I was overjoyed. *I get to talk to my mom again through Claire! This is exactly what my spiritual church means when they say that we're all one!*

"Mom, you know I have a hard head. That's why you should know the best way to get through to it," I said, through Claire.

"Your mom says she can't suddenly be loud and showy just because you want her to be."

Claire was again spot-on just like she was with hardheaded. I had always tried to force Mom to be bolder than she felt comfortable being. She wouldn't park illegally to mail a disability check and I wanted her running through heaven with a bullhorn. I apologized to Mom through Claire.

"It's okay," she replied. "Your mom says she wants you to pay more attention to subtle shifts around you. She'll be in those subtle shifts."

"I understand, Mom. You hated sticking out," I said. I realized I was an absolute crazy person to expect my mom to use energy knocking over a whole book. Especially a Maya Angelou book. My mom loved poems too much.

For fifty-eight minutes, I apologized to and asked questions of my mom. I started with softball questions—I asked if I was doing a good job with her dogs ("You are. You're spoiling them.")—then moved into harder ones, like if I had done okay by settling with Bill ("Your mom said you did what she would have done. You were strong, yet fair.").

Every word Claire channeled let me know Mom was proud of me, both in the way I took care of her and the overall adult woman I'd become. My mom's channeled words let me know she was floating on a cloud of unconditional love and even though I was stuck on earth, for a while, it was just the two of us again.

"We only have a few moments left," Claire said, gently letting me know that talking to heaven is time-limited much like talking to someone in prison. I finally dared to ask the one question that mattered most.

"What does my mom want me to do about what happened with my brother?"

"Your mom said to invite your brother over for her Soul Food Sunday tradition and everything will be fine," Claire said, then chuckled as if channeling my mom's joy at the thought. "Mom says to save her a seat at the table," she added.

Soul Food Sunday Tradition?

A seat at the table?

My mom told me she was dying over a chicken cheesesteak; she had no soul food tradition. The closest thing was the one time she "made" collard greens from a can. Growing up, because of her double shifts, we rarely ate as a family. I wouldn't know which seat at the table to save.

What should I do?

I did what my mom would have done. I thanked Claire immensely, then hung up.

Really, what was the alternative? Ask her who the hell she was talking to? Ask her if she thought we all looked alike after death? Suggest she take a psychic diversity class? Claire had handed me a soul food stereotype and taken me for my money. All I could do was laugh. Claire had inadvertently taught me just how bad my grief had become. Being a grieving daughter and avoiding humans because they said such stupid shit was so much of my identity that I'd briefly forgotten about my other identities that make people say stupid shit.

I laughed because I wasn't upset at holiday dinner invitations or at myself for crying. I was simply upset at regular old ignorance. I hadn't felt that normal in months! I phoned a good friend, one I hadn't spoken to since I'd been avoiding dumping my pain on people who couldn't understand.

"Can you believe that heifer? I waited four months to talk to my mom," I said.

"Girl, I am *dying* over here," my friend said and, miraculously, didn't apologize for saying she was dying. "Did you really think your mom was going to talk to a stranger if she hasn't even talked to you?"

And of course, a good friend will also tell you that it's insane to be jobless and spending used-car-type money on psychics. That just like Los Angeles has celebrity oncologists, it probably also has superstar therapists.

"I'm going to find a real therapist. Not Claire's fake ass," I said after Byron cautiously asked how the session went. He didn't ask for particulars on how Claire's call had catapulted me into seeing a therapist, something he and my grief websites both had suggested numerous times. Byron simply said, "Thank you, Jesus!" like he was also channeling my mom.

17

Flipped Photos and Permission

Logically, the advice to talk through my grief with someone had always seemed sound, but I'd learned from my foam slippers years that finding the right therapist can be time-consuming, and with no health insurance, therapist hopping gets expensive. With Claire, I was hoping for a onetime psychic grief solution with a onetime payment.

With no job, I was still very much a poor person and already felt haunted by the decision to use my mom's money for a psychic who'd mistaken her for Aunt Jemima. I was now determined to use Mom's money for only the basics in life that she'd approve of—food, shelter, and thrift clothing. Therapy to speed along a process that people said would only be helped by time seemed like a luxury. I did try a free grief group but was jealous that every single mourner was older than me and no one else there had lost a mom. In my self-made grief scale, I'd decided that the only people who had it worse than people who lost moms were parents who lost children. The person who thinks others in their grief group have it better than they do? Apparently, that's me. I quickly quit the group.

I also delayed going to the therapist because, well, grief is a sneaky son of a bitch. There were stretches where I felt I was healing, but then desolation, hurt, and anger would hit me out of nowhere. I still wasn't able to look at my mom's photos. I'd lovingly grouped them together on a makeshift altar and planned to start each day by talking to them. Then even looking at the photos hurt so badly, I'd cry. Instead of talking to them, I physically flipped the photos around so I wouldn't have to see them. It felt like a grief rock bottom: *What kind of daughter makes her dead mom face an electrical outlet?*

But in between pesky thoughts like wishing I'd die because I'd put my mom's photos in time-out, sometimes there was peace. I'd cling to that and claim I was making strides. At times, it seemed that I was. There were weeks I could do things that reminded me of Mom and not completely fall apart. For my nephew's birthday, I even mailed a big care package to my brother's home, just like the ones Mom used to send me. The care package was mailed back to me, an angry red "Return to Sender" stamped on the box.

When I saw the returned package, I fell to the floor. I lost it. I cried and cursed at the box about how evil my brother was.

"You bitch-ass motherfucker! You hate me so much you won't give a gift to your child?!"

And in that moment, yelling at a box, with rancid orange juice still in my fridge, an inner voice said, *Girl, you have enough inpatient experience to know that you are a mess right now. Just look up the therapist closest to you.* I still continued cursing at the returned box as I found Jennifer, a therapist who claimed to specialize in grief. There was nothing special about Jennifer's profile besides her office being close to my house; even if she was horrible, at least I wouldn't be out too much gas.

Jennifer's office walls were covered with photos of her throughout the years with friends and family. While she flipped through my intake forms, I looked around at snapshots of a younger Jennifer in the snow with what appeared to be her parents and thought, *I've chosen the wrong damn therapist.* A grief therapist having photos up of her loving family was rude; to me, it was like having an office full of marathon photos and a client who had lost both legs. I knew this was about to be some bullshit.

"How long ago did your mom pass?" Jennifer asked, looking up from my form.

"Four months," I said, my disapproving face scanning her photos.

"Four months. I'm sorry. That's recent."

I didn't believe her. Everyone had told me to take all the time I needed, but that was just another trite saying like, "Your mom's in a better place." None of us knew where my mom was, just like we all knew the world doesn't let you take as long as you need for grief.

"Four months is recent? According to who?" I asked.

"According to nature, studies by PhDs, and from what I see in here every day," Jennifer said.

And just from that tiny bit of validation, I broke down crying and grabbed the box of tissues. The tissues gave me comfort; knowing that others had sat in this chair and cried made me feel just a bit less alone, but still, I tried to suck my tears back. Crying at home felt debilitating, crying in supermarkets was embarrassing, but crying in front of a therapist on your first visit? That felt unbearable. It was way too vulnerable. I was afraid she'd judge me. *There has to be some grieving guideline I'm not measuring up to. Four months is too long to still cry.*

"Most people have no idea what you're feeling right now. They're damn lucky," Jennifer said.

I nodded—*God, I agreed with that*—but continued trying to hold back tears as I told her how people kept acting like losing a mom was something they could fix by not mentioning certain words or by inviting me over for dinner like I'm a charity case. That they thought such pain was fixable meant they had no fucking clue how it felt to lose such love. But, still, I didn't fully trust Jennifer. She had those damn family photos up.

"Are those your parents?" I asked, still eyeing the photo of her in the snow.

Jennifer got quiet. She turned to her wall of photos and her eyes lingered for a second. "Yep. My dad died ten years ago. He was my guardian, my protector," she said, her voice cracking. Her voice cracking made me trust her. Instantly. That was all it took. If there's a love at first sight for therapy, that was it. Her voice cracking showed me that even as a therapist with several letters behind her name, none of that knowledge shielded her from the pain she got from looking at one single photo of a father she lost ten years ago. For a moment, she was just a daughter without her parent. I felt for her. She was my people, a griever.

"Well, I guess your dad's in a better place," I said, rolling my eyes and hoping she'd get my sarcasm.

"Yep. He's always watching over me," she quipped back and rolled her eyes too.

"God wanted to bring his angel home," I said, and we continued throwing those trite death-sayings back and forth. That's literally all I did that first session, cry and complain about how people without dead parents were all insensitive pricks.

"I know people mean well, but they're still all such assholes! They all sound like robots reading from the Hallmark sympathy section," I said as Jennifer nodded in agreement.

I considered Jennifer to be the only person who understood. I'd come in and beat myself up over how I failed at everything from saving my amazing mom's life to keeping the family together. How I ruined weddings and wasted her money on psychics. How I felt my life had absolutely no purpose now that she was gone. I talked about how proud I was of my mom for finally leaving Bill, but how everything I'd done since she'd left proved that I could never carry that torch I was supposed to carry. How she was probably happy to be gone from my noncancer-curing jobless, psychic-trusting ass. That I was mad she hadn't sent me one clear sign. That even though I wanted a sign, when I saw a possible one, it still made me break down.

"I saw a cirrus cloud in the shape of my mom's church hat and I cried because it reminded me of all the times I didn't go to church with her," I said. "I'm tired of always crying. Mom wouldn't want me to be this weak."

"What's wrong with crying?"

"My mom never cried. Not even with stage 4 cancer or after her father died."

"That doesn't sound like being strong. That sounds like avoiding emotions," Jennifer said. "If your mom had thought about her own emotions more, she probably wouldn't have fallen in love with Bill. From what you told me, it seems like she tried to replace her father's love with his."

I balked at that. It seemed like Jennifer was trying to blame my mom. Another feature of my grief was that it made Mom more perfect than she already was in life. Hell, even Overtime and Double Overtime had transformed from being bitches to being another reason my mom was perfect. In death, she was not to be blamed for anything, especially not letting a man get one over on her.

"What's the worst thing that could happen if you allowed yourself more space to grieve than your mom did?"

"I don't know! I'm scared. This shit hurts so fucking bad! How are people walking through life like this? We should have fucking 'Griever' T-shirts and bumper stickers like breast cancer has! People would know to be just a little bit nicer to us!"

"Or you could treat yourself like you wish other people treated you."

I argued that I had no time for that. I was a woman who had no job and had also lost her entire family. I didn't want life to see how badly it had knocked me down or it would knock me even further. I had to push through the grief to get back to working twice as hard.

"You wouldn't understand. It's just something we have to do," I explained. "Plus, my mom did it fine," I added, again using my mom's saintliness to defend from what I saw as Jennifer's culturally insensitive take.

"Did she? If she was strong and could handle it on her own, then why did she move in with you?"

Damn. I wanted Jennifer to be wrong, but she had a good-ass point. Mom certainly didn't move in with me because she trusted me to be a five-star caretaker. She also had enough friends that she could have stayed in Philadelphia. Once she had her disability money, she could have even bought a new home for herself, but instead, she got on the economy-plus flight with me. It was one of those moments where someone makes you question a belief you hold as a fact. It wasn't one of those trite sayings about how much my mom loved me or was proud of me, it was proof. My mom had options and out of all of them, she'd chosen to come with me.

"She didn't just run away from Bill, she ran to you," Jennifer said. "She moved in with you and let you take care of her pain. Think about the love she had for you to trust you like that."

Those words broke me. I damn near emptied her tissue box.

"You're never going to not miss your mom. But, I promise, we can get to a point where it doesn't make you break down. Let's take it one day at a time. Let's concentrate on how you're going to get through your first Christmas without her."

"I just want to be alone for Christmas," I said and half-heartedly threw out the suggestion that I should go to the fasting retreat I'd thought could suck the glucose out of Mom's cancer. "I was going to force her to let herself be taken care of at that retreat," I explained. I had wanted my mom to understand what it meant to do absolutely nothing and that's all I felt like doing for Christmas.

"Then do it. Do nothing," Jennifer said. "Be gentle with yourself. Treat yourself how your mom should have treated herself more."

So I did it. I booked the trip I wanted my mom to take. It felt a bit frivolous, a bit too "Rothschild," but it also felt less scary than spending Christmas crying alone because I'd never again see Mom or her plastic Santas.

18

Massages and Badges

When I'd first read about the desert spa, I was convinced my mom and I would get more out of it than just starving away her cancer. The spa menu read like a smorgasbord of well-being, with classes that promised to teach us how to heal everything from our gut to our inner children. I'd had grand plans to show Mom there was a reason her favorite person Jesus had fasted in the desert.

The first day at the spa, I dove into those classes. *Heal me! I paid you thousands of dollars!* I did breath work with Bentley-driving moms and wrote things I wanted to release on strips of paper (*crying! grief! my brother!*) then set the paper on fire; I held on to crystals that truly felt like they were changing my vibrational state. I learned how to explain what a vibrational state was other than my usual, "You know, it's, like, your energy." I booked daily spa treatments. It is very hard to cry when someone is massaging your thighs. It was amazing.

But, at night, I'd be all alone with my thoughts. My thoughts were light-years away from adjectives like "amazing":

From now on, you'll be all alone for Christmas.

There's another family celebrating in the house your mom bought because you were too broke to save it.

Your mom died and your brother doesn't love you anymore.

And as one does when they are alone with scary thoughts at night, I'd boot up my laptop and shove those thoughts right away. I also started skipping the classes because the feeling I got from them was fleeting. What was the purpose of hugging crystals if they couldn't keep bad thoughts away for good? I was convinced the wellness plan worked for my fellow guests because they had Bentleys and could afford the soul-cleansing hundred-dollar gift shop candles. I was a broke orphan cosplaying at luxury. I started spending all day in the spa lobby—the only place with wi-fi.

I'd skip classes to practice becoming the best *Minesweeper* there ever was. I diffused digital bombs while lounging by the healing energy of a quartz lamp. In the lobby, I tried to wear a busy face, *don't bother me*. That didn't work because I was a first-timer at colonics and people got concerned about my absences from class; they wanted to make sure my intestines and I were okay. When I assured people I was fine, my fellow guests still wanted to trauma bond over the colonic process because, well, I'm actually not sure. My theory is that they had to be so rich and plastic surgery perfect in their regular lives that part of the spa luxury was being able to admit they use the toilet.

Talking loudly with Botoxed ladies about my daily shits became a class I hadn't signed up for but was forced to take. Once they started talking, they didn't tend to stop because we were in the desert and deserts are boring. Also because, unlike me, they'd taken the pledge to stay off their electronic devices as much as possible.

"I wish I could starve myself at home," Hannah, a repeat guest, said to me. She sighed as I continued planting flags on my *Minesweeper* board. I was envious of Hannah's ability to always say her thoughts out loud without worrying that other people didn't want to hear them. I was also envious of her whole entire life; I'd forgotten a jacket and stayed cold because the ones in the spa store cost three hundred dollars. Hannah had remembered her jacket but still bought the spa jacket in both colors because she couldn't decide between the two.

"You don't like yoga?" Hannah asked after I told her that colonic side effects weren't the reason I'd skipped classes. I didn't tell her I was playing video games, afraid I'd seem unrefined. I did explain that I was no good at yoga, which was very true.

"Well, that's why you do it, to get better at it," she said, but I didn't try again. I didn't come out to the desert to fail at more things that would keep me up at night.

Every night Hannah would see me in the lobby and give me the same look of disappointment my mom gave me when I told her I was no longer following Christianity. Hannah would share the wisdom she'd gotten out of the classes and then she would, like me, sit in the lobby online. Unlike me, Hannah had found there were other things in Apple's new app store besides games. While I was battling angry birds, on her phone she had a *Vision Board* app and on her vision board, she had photos of cars she wanted to drive, trips she wanted to take, and adjectives she wanted to be. Hannah told me she came to the spa every season and after the day's classes, she took time at night to vision her perfect next season.

Hannah had just admitted that she had a life where she could afford to go to the spa every season—and enough free time to do it—but yet before she slept in her Tempur-Pedic spa bed, she imagined how her life could be even better than all that? I thought, *That's exactly what I wanted my mom to absorb from this spa and Los Angeles*, the feeling that sometimes ripples down from the mansions: that you deserve the best in life and shouldn't care what others think about you for wanting it.

I also thought, *Damn, these rich ladies don't just throw money at sage and have it instantly cure and cleanse their lives?* I'd done vision boards, but just hung them up and forgot about them, thinking the construction board would work its magic while I slept. Meanwhile, Hannah was working double spa shifts on visions like "Bali trip" and "underwater massage."

I decided I was stronger than Hannah. She hadn't just buried a mom. I would beat her at the new game she'd shown me. I replaced my digital birds with sliding dreams around a vision board.

My dreams were very basic: I wanted to feel normal again, to have a job that paid the bills, to carry my mom's torch by doing community service, and to hear from my brother. When I went to save my visions, the app only let me save one without payment. I was paying thousands to starve myself, but wasn't paying $9.99 for dreams, so I tried to narrow down my list to one.

If I really have only one thing I could accomplish in this next season of my life, what would it be? It wouldn't be a job. I didn't really care if I traveled; I'd had enough airport security stress over the past months to last a lifetime. I didn't even really want to do community service; communities meant people, and I still wasn't keen on most of them. All I wanted was my family back.

I wanted my brother. I wanted to keep the promise he and I had made to Mom while she took her last breaths, that we would take care of each other.

The scary emotions started popping up again, those terrified thoughts of how reconciling with him was never possible because somehow God had determined that I was a failure. I forced myself to sit with them as my therapist, Jennifer, had suggested. I learned I'm no good at just sitting quietly and letting anyone talk shit to me, even my own brain. I started talking back to my negative thoughts. I cursed at them like I cursed at the box my brother returned. Even though I kept my cursing quiet, my mom would have been very embarrassed.

"Okay, bitch, I hear you," I'd say aloud when bad thoughts popped up. "Yes, you're right. My mom's dead and my brother hates me. But I can try to fix one of those things, so please shut the hell up."

That was the overwhelming thought when it came to my brother: I could still try to fix it.

But what if you fail, like you did with your mom?

Bitch, again, if you don't shut up. I didn't fail. My mom chose to come with me.

In the boring desert, I was locked in my room with nothing but time. I talked back to my thoughts for hours because dammit, Hannah doesn't get to have a better life than me. It got easier the more I kept at it. I realized my brother had stopped me from making a mistake. That just like our mom had tried to use Bill's love to replace her father's, I had tried to slide him and his family into the hole her death had left.

I wasted a ton of money by skipping out on the classes and

staying in my room plotting out a path to reconcile with Jack, but by the end of my stay, I had a plan. I decided since I had no way to call him, I'd travel to Philadelphia and hit him with a surprise visit, just like I'd done with Mom. I left the desert feeling lighter. For the first time in months, I felt I had some control over my own mind.

⸻

A few days after I left the spa, two cops rang my doorbell as I was looking up flights to Philadelphia.

What the hell? Was this a reverse manifestation? Was the vision board giving me the opposite of what I wanted because I didn't pay $9.99?

I opened my door cautiously. The cops told me they had been watching my house. I wondered what the hell for. They didn't tell me, instead they interrogated me:

Was I home all day on Christmas? Yes.

Did I see anything suspicious? No.

Could they search my yard? Yes. (I wanted to say no to that last one while adding a firm "not without a search warrant," but actually saying no to two men with guns proved harder than saying it in my head.)

"Was anyone with you on Christmas Day?" one cop asked. I told him I was alone. That made him skeptical. He raised his eyebrow.

"You don't have family?"

"Nope."

I thought admitting something so sad to a stranger would make him back off, but it seemed to make the cop more suspicious.

"Your neighbor said you put suitcases in your trunk minutes

after my partner arrived to investigate," he said, not telling me what he or his partner were investigating. He stared at me as if he expected an answer even though telling me my neighbors had seen me with suitcases wasn't exactly a question. I glanced at the homes that had a view of my driveway, wondering which of my neighbors had tipped the cops off that I dared to get in my own car the day after Christmas.

"I thought that was just so odd," they'd probably told the 911 operator. "People like her are usually home cleaning up after their traditional Christmas soul food dinners."

I finally gathered the courage to ask the cops what they were investigating.

"A homicide," the talkative red-haired cop said. He told me after the suspects had fled the murder scene, they parked by my house. "Do you know why these guys would choose your house *out of all these houses* they could have parked next to?" he asked while showing me a photo of two Black men. And just like that, the peace I felt from the spa was gone. Officer Smith was a reminder that no matter how much I vision-boarded the direction of my life, neither my mom nor I would ever know the freedom to live as a spa lady. In death, some psychics will still see us as a stereotype and in life, apparently being the only Black person on a Los Angeles block meant I must have something to do with a murder.

"I have no idea who those guys are," I said. "I was at a spa making vision boards," I added, thinking that a cop in Southern California had surely heard of those.

He shifted his stance and tapped his thigh over and over with his fingertips. His fidgeting made me nervous, but more than that, it had started to piss me off.

"You went to a spa for Christmas?" he asked.

I wanted the cops gone, just like the negative thoughts I shooed away that kept me up at night. *Do something about it*, I thought.

"Yes, I went to a spa for Christmas. I'm dying," I said.

The cop held my gaze for a few uncomfortable moments, but he also held his mouth closed, so I added, "I'm really sorry. I can't help you with your investigation. Sorry." I asked for his card and closed my door with him still on my steps.

Okay, admittedly, politely telling a cop I had an expiration date and closing the door might not seem like much, especially with those two "sorries" I wedged in there before I got to the actual door-closing part. Still, I was proud. I saw myself as a tiny, if apologetic, freedom fighter reclaiming what Hannah had taught me was important: to take time to think about my own damn needs. I was also combining that priority with the knowledge I'd recently acquired—that everyone, even homicide detectives, gets uncomfortable when the topic suddenly switches to death. As I saw it, telling them I was dying wasn't a lie; we all are dying, we all have limited time on this earth. The more time I spent talking to him, the less time I had to focus on my healing and making amends with my brother.

I knew what my mom would have done with the cops, still I did the opposite. She would probably invite the cops in for coffee after chastising me for closing the door. "You can't do what those white kids do," she'd say, explaining that by my closing the door, they were sure to find some reason to arrest me. Still, I was scared Mom's words were right. I wanted my brother to validate that I'd done okay.

I thought, *Maybe I don't need to work two times as hard to reconcile with Jack by traveling all the way to Philly.* Growing up in 1990s Philly while wearing saggy jeans meant my brother was an expert in police encounters. I decided I'd reach out to him and let him know I needed his protection, that I was done being the big, bossy postgrief sister that made him block my number. I headed back over to the app store and texted him using an app that bypassed his block by spoofing my phone number.

It's your sister. I'm getting arrested. Text me back!

With the help of several more years of therapy since sending that text, I now recognize those words as emotional blackmail: *Something bad is going to happen to me if you don't do what I want!* Telling Jack I was getting arrested was a bigger technical lie than telling the cops I was dying. Actually, I somewhat wanted the cops to arrest me; I'd hire the best lawyer, sue the hell out of them and never have to worry about finding a job again. Still, I don't regret telling my brother I was in imminent danger. I was scared he'd ignore anything less. I knew that if my brother didn't reply to a police problem, it meant I was as dead to him as our mom was. If that was the case, I'd have to learn to accept that our relationship could never fully be repaired. Still, I had to try. Just like I would gladly give up my house and everything I owned to have my mom alive one more day, my brother was alive and I was losing days with him. Nothing else mattered.

Still, I looked up things to mail to his house if he ignored my text. I'd even not put my return address on the box this time so he couldn't send it back. To stop the incoming spiral of whether he'd respond or not, I searched the internet for gifts to send enemies. I settled on a box full of exploding glitter that smelled like "liquid ass."

19

Reconciliation and Rotary Phones

Jack: You're getting arrested? You serious??

replied that I hadn't *technically* been arrested *yet*. I didn't want to give him certainty or he might not text back.

Jack: Where's Byron?
Me: I started seeing a counselor and she told me to think about myself . . . sooo I asked him to move out.
Jack: What?
Me: Yep. And trust me, he didn't seem too upset, lol. But yeah, I'm alone. All alone. Possibly being arrested.

I didn't tell him that Byron seemed ready to bounce once I told him my brother's entire family was moving in. Lies of omission combined with emotional blackmail turned out to be the winning combo to get my brother to unblock my number so we could stop texting and talk.

When he called, my brother was, as expected, happy to share my anger toward the cops' holiday intrusion and eager to share his best practices to ensure they didn't arrest or further question me. Of course, many of Jack's instructions were precisely the opposite of what I'd already done, like "Don't let them search anywhere," but, still, I thanked him for his wisdom.

We talked for a bit. Surface, boring talk. Talk that lets you side-step that you haven't talked in months. Weather. My nephew. Sports teams I knew nothing about but acted like I did because I didn't want to stop talking. When he sounded ready to hang up, I asked, "Do you know if Mom's mad at me? She didn't invite me over for Christmas this year."

"I don't know. She invited me," he said. "We had a good time. She looked a bit ashy, though."

After I fell out at his cremation joke, I cut through the surface bullshit. I apologized for being a pain-in-the-ass big sister. I apologized for making him feel like moving in with me was the only way he could properly honor our mom. I told him that my therapist made me realize that the only way through grief was to face it. How I learned I couldn't fix it by moving pieces—or my brother's whole entire family—around to hide the broken parts. That I honestly had thought that moving him in would return my life to normal.

"You paid a therapist for that?" he asked, explaining that he got the same lesson for free from his wife. "She said adjusting to a new city while also grieving was the dumbest shit she'd ever heard." He laughed. He told me that almost everyone else told him the exact same thing. And that, just like me, he got angry at them for suggesting he was making the wrong decision.

"Your anger must have been really bad," I said. "I mean, damn, you ain't never been so mad at me that you sent back a present."

"Oh shit! I didn't do that. You must have sent it to my old address. I moved," he added, explaining that he'd used his half of Mom's disability money to put a down payment on a house. His family had moved into a fixer-upper.

"That's exactly what you should have done," I said.

"Yeah, I think that's what Mom would have wanted," he said, letting me know that he was still grappling with the pull to make every decision one that Mom would approve of.

I cautiously suggested that, instead of moving permanently, we make plans at least to gather for Christmas next year.

"That way, if the cops knock, I'll at least have you as an alibi," I said.

He said he'd love for me to see his new home, and that I'd need to bring an extra Christmas present. "In a few months, you'll have a new niece," he said. His wife was pregnant with Mom's first granddaughter.

"Well, that settles it, Mom clearly loved me more than you. She stayed alive for all my kids' births," I said.

"Yoooo," he replied, bursting into laughter at his happily childless sister.

"Let's start Mom Mondays," I said, partly because I love consonance, but primarily because I wanted a reason to talk to him weekly. For Mom Mondays, I suggested we call or text each other and share memories like we did when Mom was passing. It'd be like our own private cross-country memorial. He agreed and for the next four weeks, my brother and I switched off Mondays and texted each other with mom memories.

> **Me:** Remember how Mom found a blind dog and named him Sam after some dude in the Bible?
>
> **Jack:** Remember how Mom accidentally rented a porn for us? *Crocodile Undees* was the first time I saw boobs.
>
> **Me:** Remember how Mom shed one last tear to tell us she loved us?

One Monday, I forgot to text him, caught up in a new TV writing job that demanded most of my days, nights, and weekends. I was back to the Hollywood version of Mom's Overtime, arriving early and staying late all while working twice as hard to prove my worth. I claimed to be a person who wanted to spend more time with loved ones but I had morphed back into the version of me who anxiously drove to work on little sleep, wondering if this would be the twelve-hour day that broke me. Stuck in traffic, I'd scout out bridges I could live under when everything fell apart. I forgot to slow down to do things like calling my brother. I was almost back to the "normal" I was before Mom had passed.

But, to be honest, the Mom Mondays idea was good in theory, but I should have set up more ground rules. When grief finally ceases being a daily feeling, it's jarring to get random texts about your dead mom. Network-friendly sitcom jokes were hard to conjure up when I'd start the day with a text reminding me about her last tear or the Christian poems she'd never get to publish.

Me: My therapist said I should stop this shit.

Jack: I know you didn't just pass on Mom! I know you didn't just pass your turn. This isn't a game show!

———

As months went by and my niece was closer to being born, most of Mom's belongings were still in the garage. I had stuffed everything from her socks and work ID to all her medical records in cardboard moving boxes and stacked them against the wall. I'd even piled other boxes on top of her boxes, hoping that hiding her things from view would make them somehow magically disappear. While I'd once felt bad about having Mom's photos face a corner, the last things she touched were housing spiders because I was afraid even glancing at items my mom once held in her hands would pull me into a spiral I couldn't escape. I walked through my garage with metaphorical hands over my ears and closed eyes: *Lalala, I can't see you, grief boxes!* I decided my mom was so kind, she liked being a sanctuary for spiders.

When my brother and I weren't speaking and I'd spend days praying I'd get hit by a truck, I relished the thought of him having to clean out my house. He'd get the news my body was under a tractor trailer and feel the grief of losing me combined with the guilt over blocking my number. Just when he thought he couldn't hate himself more, he'd find a box with Mom's socks. I knew, unlike Mom, I'd find a way to send him a heavenly sign: *Yeah, it was me who left you to clean both me and Mom's shit.* Now that Jack and I had reconciled,

I knew I didn't want him to go through what we'd gone through drunk on Mom's floor. I also didn't want him to donate all my things to a thrift store because I had some nice stuff and with two kids, he could use it.

I'll break Mom's stuff up into manageable chunks and only go through five items at a time, I thought. I went past the harder stuff—get well and condolence cards, hospice records—and straight to the clip earrings I'd bought her for Christmas. I put them in a donation pile for some other lucky torn-lobe lady to find; I congratulated myself for technically getting through ten things as the five earrings were in pairs.

Jack: Mom's granddaughter is here.

My brother had attached my niece's photo to the text. She had deep brown eyes to match her skin and the standard *Where the hell am I?* look that most newborns have in their first photos. I couldn't wait to see her chubby cheeks in person but I was terrified to ask my boss for a three-day weekend. I knew he was going to say no, then fire me for even asking; in Hollywood, I've seen many people dismissed for lesser infractions than wanting to meet a new niece. For days, I thought about waiting to tell my brother I'd meet my niece at Christmas. Then I remembered I had watched my mom die and therefore was no longer allowed to be afraid of things like bosses. He couldn't kill me, he could simply fire me and I'd already managed to care for myself and my mom when I didn't have a job. I decided if I got fired, I'd take it as a sign that my mom really did want my brother and me to live together and I'd move in with my brother's family and split their cheap Philly mortgage.

Losing a mother doesn't give you much, but it gives you the ability to start time-off requests with, "Hey, my mom died and I'd like to meet her first granddaughter . . ." Of course, my boss said yes to that. I quickly realized that even thinking of spending more time in the city Mom and I once called home was just as scary as her boxes.

In the days leading up to my trip, I looked up ways to keep sane and busy in Philly, distractions to avoid the hard memories. Perhaps because big tech knows everything I type on my computer, the search results included a very Philly way to talk to dead people and it wasn't through Jesus, a message board, or a psychic. There was a temporary art installation: a booth in a Philadelphia park with a disconnected rotary phone for speaking to loved ones who have passed on.

> **Me:** Have you seen Mom in any dreams yet?
> **Jack:** No. She loves you more, I get it.
> **Me:** Nope! She ain't said shit to me either! When I get to Philly, you're coming to the park and talking on this phone I found. We're going to talk to Mom!

In Philadelphia, my brother's fixer-upper house was crowded with women helping my sister-in-law tend to my new niece. Being the only childless one, I had nothing to add to their helpful tips about raising a new life. As they talked, I let my niece grasp my finger over and over.

"Wow, you're cute and strong," I said in a bouncy baby voice. Then, my childless ass realized there's not much else you can do with a newborn niece except shut up so she can sleep. My brother and I got in his car and headed out to the death phone, leaving the other women to bond over my niece's birth and the substances that came out of their bodies. It was the first time Jack and I had been alone since my trip home for Mom's memorial. We were silent for a bit. I noticed my brother's eyes were filling with water but he was trying to hide it.

"It's scary having a new baby without Mom," Jack said, merging onto the freeway that would take us to the phone.

"I can't even imagine."

"When Jay was born, she was always there to correct me if I did one thing wrong," my brother said before adding, "You know Mom taught me to change a diaper before Jay was born? Had me rubbing diaper cream all over your old dolls' butts."

"See, that's the type of fun memory we were supposed to text each other with. Not her last tear," I said.

He turned the tables and reminded me that my supposed texts of support had also made him sad.

"You remember trying to cheer me up with antelope?" he asked. Jack was referring to a time back in our death chore days when I texted him that it's not our fault coping with loss is so hard.

Me: Humans are natural hunter-gatherers. Growing up, if we needed dinner, we'd have to help Mom hunt an antelope. And we'd know, from watching other families hunt antelope, that it's possible to die when hunting antelope. We'd know that life can be gone in the blink of an eye because we'd have already seen so many families die via antelope hunting. Death would be something it's impossible to pretend only happened to others.

Jack: Damn, that's what you took out student loans to learn? No wonder your ass can't keep a job.

My brother pulled into a parking space near the phone installation. It was the same park where my mom busted her ass while teaching me to skate. The old-school rotary phone was bone-colored, just like the basic model Mom had in the kitchen back when we were growing up. A fence surrounding the phone had over a hundred brightly colored ribbons attached to it, each with the name of a loved one who had passed on. I read a few of the names and started to cry. I pulled out the letter to my mom that I'd written on the plane to avoid looking down at the city.

Dear Mommy:

First and foremost giving thanks to . . . Psych! See how I'm trying to fool you into talking to me by starting off like I was a Christian? Okay, I'll get serious.

All my life, I've been wanting to hoard you. Thank you for trusting me enough to let me do that in your final weeks. Thank you for letting me care for you. I wasn't perfect, but I think you finally saw how much I love you and how capable you raised me to be. According to all the women gathered around your new granddaughter, that's what moms want most: to know they've done right by their babies.

Thank you for trusting me with your four-legged babies. Belle and Candi don't like the beach, but in good news, Woody hasn't tried to eat them in weeks. Last weekend, the dogs were all enjoying the backyard and a butterfly landed on Candi's nose. I thought, *Wow, this has to be a sign from my mom.* Then, the butterfly flew over to Woody and he ate it, so I don't think the butterfly was you. Or that's what I tell myself, so I don't have another memory that I cry over. Don't worry, though; I'm not crying as much. *I'm fine, just fine!* Not great, but I'm fine. If I wasn't, I'd tell you because you probably have some healing power up there that my vision board cannot yet tap into.

Your co-workers miss you. I'd shoved most of their condolence cards in a garage box, sure they would only contain the *your mom's in a better place* sayings that I hated. Before this trip, I forced myself to read a few cards. I saw that though you always tried to smile through the pain, some of your co-workers knew your secrets. One of them even wrote, "I'm so grateful your mom let you take care of her and finally rest. She needed to rest." People cared about you more than your ability to outwork everyone else. Also—Haha! No one wrote anything mean about going on a California vacation! I was right!

I started rereading the BCB. (Don't worry, I plan on

shredding it; I know even in death you don't want your Social Security number in the trash.) The first BCB page I read was one of Crystal's pleural catheter reports. The bottom of the report had a series of yes and no checkboxes. Crystal had checked off only one yes; it was under "Has patient ever fallen?" Below the yes box, Crystal had also written: "Patient denies falling." Instead of breaking down, I smiled. I get it; your life didn't allow you the luxury of ever letting anyone know you were weak. I smiled because I think more than the chewed-up butterfly, Crystal's note was you talking to me, telling me you'd fallen before you'd moved in with me. Maybe you know how badly I still feel at times for not being a perfect caretaker and for leaving you alone for cheesecake. You probably also didn't tell me you had fallen before because you knew I'd have never left your side if I'd known.

I know, I know. You want to talk about your granddaughter. If that wasn't you guiding me to Crystal's note, then I for sure know you helped God make a baby face that looks just like yours, perhaps so I'd have something new to always pull me back to Philly. When your granddaughter smiles, her eyes disappear into her cheeks just like yours did. I promise I'll be there for her as she grows up—and more than just once a year at Christmas. I want her to see in me everything she would have seen in you, most importantly, your capacity to love. If there's anything specific you want her to know, I ask that you let me hoard you a little bit more—*come to me in a dream and tell me, please!* If not, I understand. Just be ready for me to be all up under you when I see you again. I miss you so damn much, but I'm certain one day, when it's my time, you'll come into my bedroom with flowers and we'll never be apart again.

While my brother talked, I looked over the city. I didn't look away, afraid that a rogue memory would take over my emotions. The city contained more than just our pain. Once my niece could do more than lie on her back and grip fingers, I wanted to show her everything Mom and I did as well as those things we never got to do.

My brother finished his call, and we got back in the car to head to his far corner of the city.

As he drove down the freeway, he pointed outside of his window at a city landmark.

"Look," he said, pointing to the neon sign atop the hospital where our mom used to work.

I flipped it the bird. "We won! We had her last!" I shouted out the window, then Jack sped off while we laughed in union, still the heathen kids my mom raised.

Epilogue

My mom told me she was dying over fifteen years ago. I never thought I'd survive fifteen years without her.

The first year after she passed, every calendar date was a new enemy. New Year's Eve wasn't a fresh start, but the end of "the last year Mom was alive." Mother's Day was a brutal holiday designed to torture people with dead moms. June wasn't the start of summer, but the month she took her last breath. My mom was born in Breast Cancer Awareness Month and died in Cancer Survivor Month. I always thought that was doubly cruel.

I no longer curse out my calendar while tracking the days I've been without my mom, but there's also a touch of self-consciousness for admitting I'm doing okay—good even—despite losing her. I'm afraid people will think that grief can been cured. That it doesn't still hurt when I see pink key chains. That I don't wonder if the newest cancer drug on my TV would have helped her. That I still fear fully cleaning out her garage boxes. My nephew was barely six years old when I shoved her belongings into boxes, now he pays taxes and has a beard. Still, the boxes stay untouched because I'm terrified I'll find a memory that snatches me up and drags me back into the depths of grief. But that's where I am: I survived fifteen years and can take Mother's Day on the chin like a champ, but I'm paralyzed that her clip earrings can emotionally whip my ass.

As I hit middle age without Mom, there are so many talks I wish we could have. I'd love to tell her she was right—I do understand what it's like to have knees that sound like Rice Krispies. I'd apologize for simply being a teen while she went through menopause because "the change," as she called it, is no joke. I'd love to tell her I've learned that self-care is deeper than good jobs, fasting spas, and once-a-year family visits. I'd love to share that I honor her not by doing exactly what I think she wants, but instead doing what I feel she often failed to—put her own needs above others'.

I miss Mom thumbing through my books' first drafts while asking if there was a job I could get that didn't involve telling all her business. I miss her feeling like a star when someone invited her to tell her story alongside mine. One time, she called me excited; a thrift shop employee had seen her on the local news and gave her a huge discount. I miss her learning that revealing our "business" and messy parts didn't mean people would judge us harshly.

I miss her way of hiding lessons in her mistakes. I wish I could think of a way to end this epilogue with a grand lesson, like when she taught me about magnetism through aluminum cans. Then I remember that I am a woman who was perfectly fine having a personal trainer lead Mom's memorial; perhaps I'm not the right person to give advice.

Still, there are things I wish I'd known fifteen years ago when I took that last trip to Mom's. I wished someone had told me lying to your mom for her own good can be fun. Mom always caught me in lies when I was young, but as an adult, I knew all her tells and weak points. Tricking my work-loving mom into thinking I had a Hollywood job while I shoveled horse shit is one of my greatest accomplishments. My lie allowed her to rest without worry.

I learned that priding myself on working twice as hard can no longer be my priority. I judge my success not through job titles but in how many loved ones pick up the phone when I call. I've learned not to hide from my friends when I'm struggling and that true ones forgive me for getting pissed at their holiday invites. A few of the ones who have lost their moms since I lost mine even admit that they now understand.

I've learned I'm the new matriarch of the family. I'm the oldest aunt, the one who doesn't understand my niece and nephew's music and makes sure my brother keeps his health in check. Like Mom, I find joy in slowing down a bit, in having rituals others may consider boring. My perfect Saturdays consist of caring for my plants or mailing care packages to my niece. Sundays? Well, the last time I've been in a church was Mom's memorial. I'm sorry, Mom, but my perfect Sunday is spent giving thanks for legal THC.

I've learned that life is easier when you remember that everyone is going through their shit. I try to be less judgmental; I give grace to people who hold up city blocks, airport lines, and park illegally. I try to smile at people for no reason. I've gone very soft and I like it.

Just like my mom worried about California, my brother worries my softness means I'll get robbed soon.

I've learned that I'll never be a cancer expert, but I can be more gentle with the words I use. I no longer believe in slogans that pressure people to "fight" and "win the battle," as if surviving illness is a measure of one's toughness. It's cancer, not a fucking boxing match. I know there is never any shame in folding if you feel you've fought enough. I also know I've reembraced the magic of hope, but I'm careful not to rely on it so much that it blinds me to reality.

My mom hasn't sent me a big sign. No lights have flickered in my home and the spirits that greeted her in death haven't dropped by to give me updates. She has, however, appeared to me in three dreams: In one, we were shopping, in the second we were watching TV, in my third and latest she was pregnant with twins from a fine-ass man. I have no idea what that last one means, but my mom looked happy as hell, despite being sixty-four and pregnant. I also wonder if maybe the celebrity psychic was right: My mom's in the small shifts, the tiny interactions that in hindsight have always led me to choose the right path. Mom was in her friend Geraldine phoning during her memorial, Mom led me to a great therapist, and she was even in the cops who gave me the spark to call my brother and reconcile.

If you're reading this and you've lost someone, I wish you all the peace in the world. I pray you reach the place I finally reached, where your loved ones' memories are much more a blessing than they are a burden. I'm rooting for you and I'm certain my mom is too. I know this because despite her not sending me a big sign, we still have our catch-up calls. When I'm still, I can hear her voice so clearly. She said if I'm going to tell all her business make sure I let other daughters and sons know that they're loved more than they can imagine. She also said I have to finally keep my promise and help her publish a poem.

Here you go, Mom.

Places

Sometimes we wonder why a loved one is not allowed more time
    with us on earth.
Sometimes we wonder why they are taken to heaven before us.
Could it be that their energy is used to open the windows of
    heaven
so that blessings can be poured out to us?
Could it be that their creativity is used to design imaginative
    dwellings
so that when we get there, we will have comfort?
Could it be that they were taken to heaven before us
so that when we get there, we will recognize a familiar face and
    voice?
To smile at us and say to us
You're here and I'm here and never again in eternity will we be
    parted.

Gwendolyn Nissel

Acknowledgments

I owe a debt of gratitude to so many people for making this book possible. Thank you, Patrik Henry Bass, for your honesty, passion, and, most importantly, for believing. Thank you, Abby West. Thank you, Anayaé Holmes. Thank you, Heather Bosch and Amy Sather.

I'm grateful for my friends who held my hand as I cried through some of the memories: Judy Reyes, Laiya St. Clair, Nadyne Hicks, and Angela Rye. I'd also like to thank Jan Miller for her passion, dedication, and for helping me find a home for my words.

I'm grateful for Karen Earl; your kindness toward my mother lives forever in my heart. I give thanks for my great therapists: Joanna S. and Barbara H.

I'm forever indebted to Melody, Porscha, Benjamin, and Skip.

A million thank-yous to my fucking amazing brother, Jack, for allowing me to put our story on paper. Thank you to Aunt Jeanette and Aunt Bea. Thank you, Uncle John, Cousin John, and Cousin

Acknowledgments

Raymond. Thank you, Mark and Ani Kertenian. Thank you to all my mom's friends and co-workers and everyone else whose love guided me. Thank you, Pepinos. Thank you to the many of you written about in these pages who have already crossed over. Please give Mom a hug.

About the Author

Angela Nissel is the author of the national bestselling comedic memoirs *The Broke Diaries* and *Mixed*. In addition to books, she is a prolific television producer/writer with *The Other Black Girl*, *Mixed-ish*, and *Scrubs* among her credits. Before Hollywood, she had a stellar career as a temp for the IRS, measured people's snores as a "sleep apnea auditor," and was a morning-shift stripper.